HISTORY NOTES
Richard Wilcox

A STUDY GUIDE TO ACCOMPANY

THE
AMERICAN JOURNEY

VOLUME TWO

TEACHING AND LEARNING CLASSROOM EDITION
BRIEF THIRD EDITION

David Goldfield

Carl Abbott

Virginia DeJohn Anderson

Jo Ann E. Argersinger

Peter H. Argersinger

William L. Barney

Robert M. Weir

PEARSON

Prentice
Hall

Upper Saddle River, New Jersey 07458

P9-DIB-097

© 2005 by PEARSON EDUCATION, INC.
Upper Saddle River, New Jersey 07458

All rights reserved

10 9 8 7 6 5 4 3

ISBN 0-13-132197-8

Printed in the United States of America

CONTENTS

Chapter 16
Reconstruction, 1865-1877

Practice Test

1. During his travels across the United States after the Civil War, Mark Twain observed that
    A) Northerners had made the memory of the war the center of their socio-political lives.
    B) Southerners were so bitter about the war's outcome that they wouldn't discuss it.
    C) Americans across the nation acted as if the Civil War had never happened.
    D) people of the South discussed the war far more often than people in the North.

2. Effects of the Civil War in the South included all of the following EXCEPT
    A) a romanticization of Robert E. Lee by many white Southerners.
    B) a recognition by most Southerners that their cause had not been a noble one.
    C) a brief period when Radical Republicans enforced voting and legal rights for ex-slaves.
    D) an insistence by many whites on maintaining economic superiority for whites.

3. The Freedmen's Bureau was established to
    A) help most southern blacks move to the North.
    B) encourage the development of multiracial churches.
    C) aid ex-slaves in adapting to socio-economic changes.
    D) provide aid for disabled veterans of the war.

4. In the early years of Reconstruction, the Freedmen's Bureau was successful at
    A) permanently securing suffrage for black males.
    B) stopping all violence committed against ex-slaves.
    C) reducing black illiteracy to below 70 percent.
    D) convincing southern whites to accept the Wade-Davis Bill.

5. General Sherman's Field Order No. 15 gave hope to blacks because it
    A) set aside plots of southern land for distribution.
    B) guaranteed all ex-slaves the right to a free education.
    C) established voting rights for black males in the South.
    D) indicated that segregation was unconstitutional.

6. Ownership of land by blacks was highest in
    A) areas that had not experienced battles during the Civil War.
    B) poorer areas of the Lower South.
    C) the area known as the "Sherman Land" during 1820-1865.
    D) the Upper South, especially Virginia.

7. The church became the center of black life for all of the following reasons EXCEPT
    A) it gave blacks an opportunity to practice skills of self government.
    B) it operated as an educational institution as well.
    C) it represented visible evidence of the progress blacks had made.
    D) it allowed them to socialize with whites.

8. The first building erected in Charleston after the war was
    A) the local bank.
    B) a black church.
    C) local seat of government.
    D) a retail/feed store.

9. _____ was the most influential AME minister of his day.
    A) James Henry Holmes
    B) Frederick Ayer
    C) Henry Mc Neal Turner
    D) Horatio Seymour

10. The Wade-Davis Bill was rendered ineffective when
    A) President Lincoln used the presidential option of a pocket veto.
    B) southern conservatives refused to enact it.
    C) radical Republicans rejected the plan as too lenient.
    D) abolitionist leaders withdrew their support for the bill.

11. Which statement would most likely have been said by a conservative Republican in 1865?
    A) "The Constitution does not grant secession, thus the South has never left the Union."
    B) "Northern hypocrisy shall never determine the destiny of the South's future."
    C) "The former Confederate states are to be treated as provinces conquered in war."
    D) "It is with no malice in our hearts that we welcome the return of our southern brothers."

12. President Johnson's Reconstruction plan included all of the following proposals EXCEPT
    A) restoration of property rights to southerners who pledged allegiance to the Union.
    B) requiring wealthier southerners to petition the president for a pardon.
    C) the insistence that restored property rights did not include the revival of slavery.
    D) the extension of voting rights to all black males, 21 or older, in the South.

13. The immediate response to President Johnson's Reconstruction plan included
    A) resistance by white Southerners to various provisions.
    B) opposition by the majority of northern Democrats.
    C) the loss of Johnson's reputation as a moderate.
    D) the call for elections in which southern blacks voted.

14. Black code laws included all of the following EXCEPT:
    A) barred Blacks from jury duty
    B) forbade Blacks from possessing firearms
    C) allowed Blacks to pursue any occupation they chose
    D) forced Blacks into labor on farms and road crews

15. Republicans in Congress became infuriated when
    A) President Johnson took a tough stand against wealthy Southerners.
    B) abolitionists lobbied for black male suffrage.
    C) southern states enacted laws that restricted freedom for blacks.
    D) they lost control of the House of Representatives in 1866.

16. Throughout his political career, Thaddeus Stevens was a consistent spokesman for
    A) implementation of state's rights.
    B) the equality and peaceful coexistence of whites and blacks.
    C) southern whites who did not wish to see their traditions altered.
    D) social separation of whites and blacks.

17. In 1866, Moderate Republicans in Congress did NOT support
    A) continuing the Freedmen's Bureau.
    B) harsh punitive measures against ex-Confederate leaders.
    C) protecting the civil rights of former slaves.
    D) promoting voting rights for former slaves.

18. The Fourteenth Amendment incorporated some of the provisions from
    A) the Thirteenth Amendment.
    B) the Civil Rights Act of 1866.
    C) American Equal Rights Act.
    D) the Civil Rights Act of 1875.

19. Congress overrode President Johnson's veto of which Act?
    A) The Civil Rights Act of 1875
    B) The Civil Rights Act of 1866
    C) The Civil Rights Act of 1871
    D) The Southern Homestead Act

20. Which statement about the Fourteenth Amendment is NOT true?
    A) It guaranteed all citizens equality before the law.
    B) It strengthened the Civil Rights Act of 1866.
    C) It was opposed by President Johnson.
    D) It guaranteed all males the right to vote.

21. The radical Republicans' goals for Reconstruction included all of the following EXCEPT
    A) the South's recognition of the consequences of defeat.
    B) the securing of the freedmen's right to vote.
    C) stopping southern states from reentering the Union.
    D) attempting to strengthen the Republican Party in the South.

22. The Tenure of Office Act attempted to
    A) dismantle state governments in the Lower South.
    B) weaken the powers of the president.
    C) guarantee the election of Republicans in the North.
    D) stop the nomination of Ulysses S. Grant for president.

23. The Fifteenth Amendment
    A) gave Congress the power to remove presidential cabinet members.
    B) officially ended slavery in the United States.
    C) established new rules for readmission of southern states.
    D) guaranteed the right of American men to vote.

24. What term was originally used in pre-Civil War New York City?
    A) Carpetbagger
    B) Scalawag
    C) Redeemer
    D) Roundhead

25. Who started the American Equal Right Association?
    A) Wendell Phillips
    B) Martha Schofield
    C) Elizabeth Cady Stanton
    D) Susan B. Anthony

When?

1. Which headline would have appeared in 1876?
    A) "Grant Steamrolls to Easy Second-Term Victory"
    B) "Congress Passes Act in Effort to Stop Klan"
    C) "Constitutional Amendment Gives Suffrage Rights to Ex-Slaves"
    D) "Hayes, Tilden Outcome Stalled in Contested Deadlock"

2. Which event happened last?
    A) Field Order No. 15 was issued
    B) Supreme Court nullified the Enforcement Act
    C) Southern blacks voted, in large numbers, for Ulysses S. Grant
    D) Fourteenth Amendment was passed by Congress

3. What is the correct order of presidential succession?
   A) Grant, Johnson, Hayes
   B) Johnson, Hayes, Grant
   C) Johnson, Grant, Hayes
   D) Grant, Hayes, Johnson

4. In which year did "Liberal Republicans" in Congress emerge as a separate party?
   A) 1866
   B) 1869
   C) 1872
   D) 1884

5. Which event happened last?
   A) Freedmen Bureau closes
   B) radical Republicans moved to oust President Johnson from office
   C) Republican civil rights advocate, Charles Sumner, died
   D) The Ku Klux Klan emerged as a force of terror in the South

Where?

Matching

Match the following people with the appropriate state.

Thaddeus Stevens	Massachusetts
Charles Sumner	Indiana
Martha Schofield	New York
William Tweed	Pennsylvania
	Louisiana
	South Carolina

Map Skills

Using Map 16-1 from your text, answer and label the following questions:

1. Draw the boundaries of the 5 new military districts.

2. Which districts had the highest number of former Confederate states?

3. Which was the first state admitted back into the Union?

4. Which was the last state admitted back into the Union?

How and Why?

1. What accomplishments did the Freedmen's Bureau make during Reconstruction?

2. Compare and contrast the White Southern perspective of end of the Civil War with that of the Black Southern perspective.

3. Describe the characteristics that define the sharecropping system.

4. During Reconstruction, what factors made the Republican Party a powerful force in all national elections?

5. What laws and amendments were passed by Congress in its effort to extend the parameters of democracy during Reconstruction?

6. Historians are divided in opinion regarding their interpretations of Reconstruction's events and outcomes. What do you feel were the events that best express the Reconstruction period? Why do you feel Reconstruction reforms were ended in 1877?

7. What factors accounted for the rise of the Republican Party in the South, and then the reemergence of the Democratic Party as the dominant power in the South?

8. W.E.B. Dubois stated that Reconstruction was a time in which, "The slave went free; stood a brief moment in the sun; then moved back toward slavery." What historical evidence supports Dubois's thesis?

9. Briefly describe the entrance of Blacks into the political arena in the South. What types of legislation did they seek to pass and why? Then briefly mention what led to their demise as officeholders.

10. Many historians feel that both the promise and disappointment of Reconstruction provided the foundation for the next 100 years of race relations in the South. In what ways is this idea true?

Chapter 17
A New South, 1877-1900

Practice Test

1. Industrialism in the New South
    A) created jobs for tens of thousands of first-time industrial wage earners.
    B) brought large-scale use of electricity to the Lower South.
    C) generally broadened the foundation of the rural economy.
    D) produced no further construction of rail lines in the South.

2. The term *Solid South* refers to
    A) reform groups that supported racial unity.
    B) the growing power of the Lower South in the national economy.
    C) the dominance of the Democratic Party in southern politics.
    D) the South's commitment to balancing the wealth in the rural economy.

3. Important emerging industries in the New South included all of the following EXCEPT
    A) textiles.
    B) tobacco in the form of cigarettes.
    C) railroad construction.
    D) processed chemicals.

4. What modern-day commodity became successful in the South by the early 1900s?
    A) Kleenex
    B) Coca-Cola
    C) Ford automobiles
    D) Hershey candy bars

5. Coca-Cola's original purpose was to cure
    A) stomach aches.
    B) ear aches.
    C) headaches.
    D) none of the above.

6. Industrialism in the New South
    A) put the South at the forefront of the national economy by the early 1900s.
    B) developed with higher wages for workers when compared to the North.
    C) barely kept pace with the booming industrial economy of the North.
    D) dramatically increased consumer spending throughout the South.

7. Which statement about educational investment in the New South is true?
   A) Southern spending on education kept pace with most rural states of the North.
   B) State governments of the South refused to allot funds for education.
   C) The federal government spent great amounts of money promoting education.
   D) Southern states tended to spend far less on education than northern states.

8. In early 1866, which city had become the central point for Northern and Western trade coming Southward?
   A) Savannah
   B) Atlanta
   C) Dallas
   D) New Orleans

9. All of the following was true about the lumber industry in the New South EXCEPT:
   A) require excessive amounts of capital.
   B) processed its raw materials onsite.
   C) left the landscape bare.
   D) displaced residents.

10. Many middle-class reformers objected to industrial labor because they disliked
    A) all labor unions that defended the rights of workers.
    B) bringing urban development to the South.
    C) the spread of socialist ideas in the Deep South.
    D) the changes it caused in individual and family life.

11. Traditional southerners felt that urban development in the South was
    A) needed to uplift the lagging culture of the South.
    B) evidence of the continuing domination of the North.
    C) a benefit to increasing participation in organized religion.
    D) a positive development in the transformation toward an industrial economy.

12. After the Civil War, farmers from the South
    A) enjoyed an increase in cotton prices.
    B) grew more food crops and less cotton.
    C) paid low prices for fertilizer and farm tools.
    D) grew more cotton, but made less money.

13. Which statement about cotton in the late 1800s of the New South is NOT true?
    A) It was often used as collateral on loans.
    B) Growing even more cotton would have bolstered sagging prices.
    C) Increasing numbers of southern farmers began to cultivate cotton.
    D) Many farmers chose growing cotton over diversification.

14. *Redeemer Democrats* represented the interests of
   A) White southerners.
   B) ex-slaves.
   C) large landholders.
   D) northern industrialists.

15. In fear of losing popular support, Redeemer Democrats
   A) supported a policy of strict regulation of the railways.
   B) sought the support of the huge number of African-American voters.
   C) backed legislation that lowered interest rates and eased credit.
   D) preached a message of regional and racial unity to whites.

16. The leaders of the Grange
   A) were Democratic representatives in the United States Congress.
   B) tended to come from the wealthier landowning class.
   C) were also involved in mobilizing the Socialist Party.
   D) aggressively backed a program that would end the credit system.

17. A major difference between the Agricultural Wheel and the Grange was
   A) the Grange supported radical policies that endorsed community ownership.
   B) the Agricultural Wheel had far fewer members.
   C) the Agricultural Wheel supported federal help for struggling farmers.
   D) the Grange lacked a foundation among landowning farmers.

18. The powerful Southern Farmers' Alliance had its origins in
   A) Texas.
   B) Georgia.
   C) Nebraska.
   D) Mississippi.

19. Which description is the best portrayal of the Southern Farmers' Alliance?
   A) A political party that challenged Redeemer Democrats in the 1880s.
   B) A consensus group that promoted the urbanization of the South.
   C) An organization founded in traditional southern values and cooperative ventures.
   D) A political lobbying group that influenced and changed federal farming policies.

20. Membership in The Alliance included all of the following EXCEPT:
   A) belief in the divinity of Jesus.
   B) salvation through economic dues.
   C) literal belief of the Bible.
   D) salvation through cooperation.

21. The Holiness movement and the Church of God were similar in the way they
    A) rejected secular evils and accepted women on an equal basis.
    B) combined religious fundamentalism with political activism on a federal level.
    C) supported religious fundamentalists as candidates for president.
    D) always refused to allow blacks to join their churches.

22. The Colored Alliance staged a strike in their effort to
    A) gain equal status within the Democratic Party.
    B) establish higher wages for cotton pickers.
    C) bring labor unions to factories in the industrial South.
    D) boycott unfair prices set by manufacturers of jute.

23. Which statement best describes the *subtreasury plan* ?
    A) Using silver, rather than gold, to back the national currency.
    B) Storing cotton in warehouses in an effort to increase cotton prices.
    C) Utilizing patronage to control key committees in state legislatures.
    D) Refusing to pay loans to protest segregation of state institutions.

24. Women in the South
    A) staged an extensive reform movement much like the movement staged by Northern women.
    B) broadened their social roles immediately following the Civil War.
    C) understood their role in southern society as paragons of virtue.
    D) none of the above.

25. The one difference between settlement houses in the North and the South was
    A) provided services for the less fortunate.
    B) women were instrumental in their success/foundations.
    C) they were privately sponsored.
    D) none of the above.

When?

1. Which event happened last?
    A) The Supreme Court issued its decision in *Plessy v. Ferguson*.
    B) The Tuskegee Institute was opened.
    C) Mississippi used literacy tests to restrict black suffrage.
    D) Race riots occurred in Atlanta.

2. Which headline would have appeared in 1906?
    A) "Bloody Racer Riot Turns Atlanta into Cauldron of Violence"
    B) "Populists Run Candidates for the First Time in Local Elections"
    C) "Farmers' Alliance Plans Large Boycott of Jute Manufacturers"
    D) "Dubois is First Negro to Earn Degree at Harvard"

3. What is the correct order of events?
    A) Atlanta Compromise address, Farmers' Alliance goes national, *Plessy v. Ferguson*
    B) *Plessy v. Ferguson*, Farmers' Alliance goes national, Atlanta Compromise address
    C) Farmers' Alliance goes national, *Plessy v. Ferguson*, Atlanta Compromise address
    D) Farmers' Alliance goes national, Atlanta Compromise address, *Plessy v. Ferguson*

4. When did the populist party emerge?
    A) 1888
    B) 1890
    C) 1892
    D) 1894

5. When was *Plessy v. Ferguson* ruled on?
    A) 1858
    B) 1866
    C) 1896
    D) 1890

Where?

Matching

Match the figure with his home state.

John Pemberton	Massachusetts
Ida b. Wells	Georgia
Lily Hammond	Wisconsin
W. E. B. Du Bois	Tennessee
Charles Macune	

Map Skills

Use Map 17-1 from your text to answer the following questions.

1. Describe the development of railroads in the South from 1859-1899.

2. Describe the economic effects of railroad development in the South.

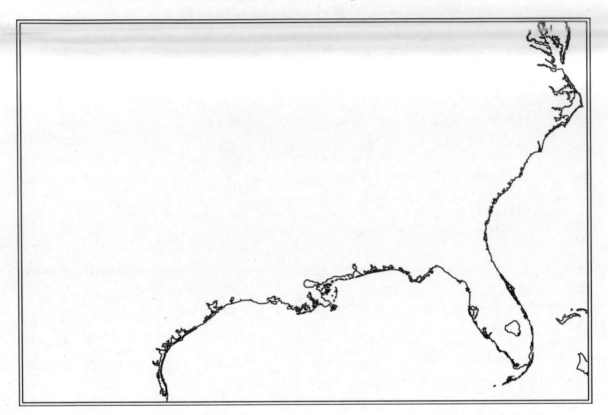

How and Why?

1. What were some major examples of the growth of southern industry in the last quarter-century of the 1800s?

2. What grievances and programs were expressed by the Southern Farmers' Alliance?

3. In what ways did conservative governments of the South take away the suffrage rights of black men?

4. Discuss the ways in which Southern women protected their regional memories of the South after the Civil War.

5. What was the Populist Party's original stance on race within their movement?

6. In what ways was the activism of female reformers in the South both progressive and reactionary?

7. Compare and contrast the views of Booker T. Washington and W.E.B. Dubois regarding strategies that would achieve social progress for African-Americans.

8. Address the following statement: "In the period 1876-1900, the South made economic progress, but experienced social polarization as well."

9. What factors accounted for the quick appeal, and then the sudden fall of the Populist Party in the South?

10. Describe the nature of the opposing forces of social reform and white supremacy in the South during the period 1880-1900.

Chapter 18
Industry, Immigrants, and Cities, 1870-1900

Practice Test

1. America proudly displayed its newest technological wonders at the Centennial Exposition in
     A) Philadelphia.
     B) New York.
     C) Detroit.
     D) St. Louis.

2. The term *gilded age* refers specifically to a time when
     A) labor unions were successfully promoting their own candidates for president.
     B) America reached a healthy balance of wealth among all social classes.
     C) shallow worship of wealth and sharp social divisions existed.
     D) Americans were migrating from the North to the South in record numbers.

3. As the size of the industrial work force grew in the late nineteenth century,
     A) working conditions greatly improved.
     B) immigration to the Northeast decreased.
     C) the number of firms in given industries shrank.
     D) ethnic urban regions experienced a golden age of prosperity.

4. Middle-class life was improved by
     A) electricity.
     B) ready-made clothing.
     C) store-bought food.
     D) all of the above.

5. Thomas Edison accomplished all of the following achievements EXCEPT
     A) inventing a telegraph that sent multiple messages on the same wire.
     B) developing the first practical use of the light bulb.
     C) creating an improved stock market ticker.
     D) being the first person to experiment with electrical energy.

6. Edison organized the building of the first electrical power plant in
     A) Philadelphia.
     B) New York City.
     C) Menlo Park, New Jersey.
     D) Springfield, Missouri.

7. The major significance of Elihu Thomson's career was his
   A) leadership of Kodak as the world's major photographic company.
   B) establishing the country's first corporate research and development division.
   C) role in creating the first commercial telegraph.
   D) use of vertical integration in dominating the oil industry.

8. An effect of the rise of corporations in America was
   A) a decrease in the amount of long-term planning by leaders of companies.
   B) shareholders were held personally responsible for corporate debts.
   C) an increase in the number of owners who became middle-management leaders.
   D) a stimulation of capital investment and technological advances.

9. Before the industrial boom of the late 1800's,
   A) labor was done by artisans who controlled the pace and output of their labor.
   B) middle-class artisans were rare in the Northeast.
   C) labor was entirely organized by middle-management employees.
   D) monopolies harmed economic growth in the urban areas of the North.

10. An example of *vertical integration* was
    A) John Rockefeller's mergers with other oil companies.
    B) Andrew Carnegie's belief in helping his working-class laborers.
    C) Gustavas Swift's control of all aspects of meat-packing.
    D) J.P. Morgan's belief in the "gospel of wealth."

11. The aggressive tactics of John D. Rockefeller were supported by his
    A) strong support for the Knights of Labor.
    B) financial alliance with investment banker, J.P. Morgan.
    C) belief in the "gospel of wealth."
    D) refusal to adapt new technological advances.

12. An industrial owner who practiced *horizontal integration*
    A) aimed to appease labor.
    B) bought out competitors in the same industry.
    C) invested in a wide variety of industries.
    D) believed that monopoly was destructive to economic needs.

13. The pioneer of horizontal integration was
    A) James B. Duke.
    B) Gustavas Swift.
    C) George Pullman.
    D) John D. Rockefeller.

14. Automated cigarette manufacturing was pioneered by
   A) James B. Duke.
   B) Gustavas Swift.
   C) George Pullman.
   D) John D. Rockefeller.

15. One disadvantage, for American workers, of the rise of corporations was
   A) corporations now controlled the conditions and nature of work.
   B) fewer jobs were provided because of automation.
   C) the government's decision to cut off all immigration.
   D) corporations refused to work in coalition with investment banks.

16. Eastern European immigrants made up the bulk of what industry?
   A) meat packing
   B) railways
   C) steel manufacturing
   D) oil refineries

17. One effect of workers being required to work long hours was
   A) an increase in hourly wages.
   B) larger numbers of workers becoming artisans.
   C) a decrease in deaths and injuries on the job.
   D) a disruption of workers' family lives.

18. The use of *sweatshops* was most common in
   A) coal mining.
   B) the garment industry.
   C) Andrew Carnegie's steel plants.
   D) new factories of the West.

19. By 1900, legislative acts that regulated the horrors of child labor were
   A) successful at ending the practice in the United States.
   B) passed by state legislatures in 90% of the states.
   C) supported by most industrialists of the East.
   D) not effectively enforced by authorities.

20. Which statement about women and children in the work force is *not* true?
   A) The trend toward deskilling provided more jobs for women and children.
   B) Conditions were hard for women and children, but they received the same pay
      as men.
   C) Between 1870 and 1920, women and children in the workplace increased
      dramatically.
   D) Most women and children worked due to poor economic conditions

21. On average, men made $16 a week compared to women's wages of _____ per week for the same job.
    A) $4
    B) $6
    C) $10
    D) $12

22. In the early 1900s, rare professional opportunities were available to women as
    A) lawyers and physicians.
    B) teachers and physicians.
    C) clerical workers and teachers.
    D) lawyers and clerical workers.

23. The purpose of the settlement house movement was to
    A) help the working poor by providing education and social services.
    B) promote labor candidates for national political offices.
    C) involve Congressmen in community service.
    D) support the cooperative ideals of the Knights of Labor.

24. Andrew Carnegie stated a differing view of the Gospel of Wealth by expressing that
    A) socialists and capitalists should cooperate in labor negotiations.
    B) settlement houses were ineffective at addressing the needs of the poor.
    C) the government was entirely responsible for poor living conditions.
    D) the affluent class should return some of their wealth to working class communities.

25. Which statement would most likely have been said by a believer in Social Darwinism?
    A) "Charity and the goodness of the affluent heart will lead this era of progress."
    B) "The government must regulate business if we are to help the working poor."
    C) "The laws of nature dictate the conditions of life for both rich and poor."
    D) "Nature's mighty laws tell us that the rich must donate endowments for the poor."

When?

1. Which event did NOT happen in the 1890s?
    A) President Cleveland interceded in the Pullman strike.
    B) Guerrilla warfare raged in the hills during the Homestead Strike.
    C) The Knights of Labor experienced their largest membership.
    D) General Electric opened its research facility plant.

2. Which event happened last?
   A) The Erdman Act established mediation in railroad labor disputes.
   B) Policemen and workers were killed when a bomb explodes at Haymarket Square.
   C) Clay Frick hired scabs to break the Homestead Steel strike.
   D) Eugene Debs lead workers' protests in the Pullman strike.

3. Which labor dispute happened first?
   A) Haymarket Square Riot
   B) the Homestead Steel Strike
   C) the Great Uprising in the railway industry
   D) the Pullman strike

4. The Hull House was founded in
   A) 1886.
   B) 1894.
   C) 1897.
   D) 1889.

5. In which decade did John D. Rockefeller form Standard Oil?
   A) 1870-1879
   B) 1880-1889
   C) 1890-1899
   D) 1900-1909

Where?

Matching

Match the following figures with their home states.

Thomas Edison	Louisiana
Elihu Thomson	Illinois
John D. Rockefeller	Pennsylvania
Daniel Hale Williams	New York
Ellla Russell	New Jersey

Map Skills

Use Map 18-2 from your text to answer and label the following questions.

1. In 1900, what was the largest city west of the Rocky Mountains?

2. What was the largest city south of St. Louis?

3. By 1900, what was the largest city in the U.S.?

4. By 1900, which city was larger, St. Louis or Washington, D.C.?

5. By 1900, which city was larger, San Francisco or Los Angeles?

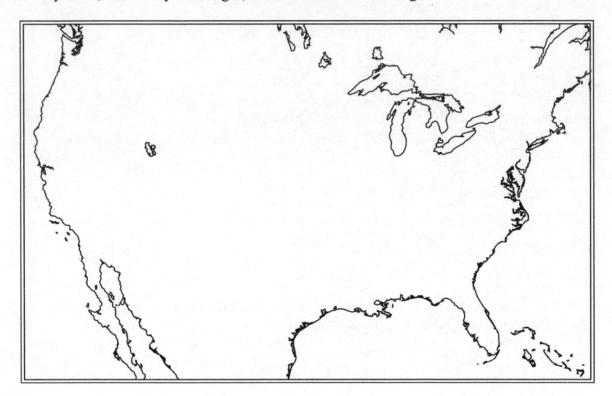

How and Why?

1. Describe examples of both *vertical* and *horizontal integration.*

2. In what ways did labor conditions change for the working class in the 50 years after the Civil War?

3. What conditions were similar and different for new immigrants and blacks in urban areas?

4. How did nativist groups attempt to halt the mixture of culture that came to the United States in the period 1880-1910?

5. What circumstances led to the sudden rise and fall of the Knights of Labor?

6. Compare and contrast the philosophies and tactics of the Knights of Labor, the American Federation of Labor, and the International Workers of the World? Why, in the long run, did one group succeed while the other two failed?

7. What social developments reveal the emergence of a predominant middle-class culture in the United States?

8. Address the following statement: "Despite the great wealth produced by the industrial boom, class divisions in America were sharply divisive in the period 1880-1910."

9. How did the newly developed immigrant neighborhoods provide a familiar and supportive environment for its inhabitants?

10. Support one of the following positions:
    "New immigrants were assimilated into mainstream American culture."
    "New immigrants adjusted to mainstream American culture."
    "New immigrants adjusted to American culture and contributed to its diversity."

Chapter 19
Transforming the West, 1865-1890

Practice Test

1. Which statement best describes the cultures of the tribes that lived throughout the West?
    A) Most tribes had a difficult time surviving without the benefits of technology.
    B) A wide spectrum of tribes had successfully adapted to a variety of environments.
    C) The tribes shared the same rituals in regions from the Mississippi to the Pacific.
    D) Village Indians were having a difficult time living within the balance of nature.

2. Pueblo society was noted for its
    A) intensive agriculture and unified community goals.
    B) nomadic hunting and herding of sheep.
    C) reliance on living in small, isolated clans.
    D) hunting of buffalo on the Great Plains.

3. All of the following tribes lived on the Great Plains EXCEPT the
    A) Cheyennes.
    B) Chinooks.
    C) Arapahos.
    D) Sioux.

4. Extracting food and medicines from plants as well as eating _____ supplemented the diets of the Indian groups that lived in the Great Plains.
    A) grasshoppers
    B) rabbits
    C) mice
    D) buffalo

5. A common element among all tribes of the West was their
    A) belief in the same gods.
    B) use of teepees as an efficient living unit.
    C) nomadic wandering that relied on searching for dietary supplements.
    D) belief that nature was to be shared and not privately owned.

6. What event in 1848 started a huge influx of whites into Indian territory?
    A) the Sand Creek Massacre
    B) passage of the Homestead Act
    C) the discovery of gold in Indian territories
    D) the Battle of Little Big Horn

7. All of the following factors resulted in many Indian deaths on the Great Plains EXCEPT
    A) the spread of smallpox.
    B) starvation caused by decimation of the buffalo herds.
    C) the Indians' lack of immunities to new diseases.
    D) Indians always refusing to move to new land.

8. What statement best describes General Philip Sheridan's views on Indian resistance?
    A) "There would be no conflict without the stubborn nature of the Indians."
    B) "Looking at the situation, how could anyone expect Indians to react any other way?"
    C) "The American military has always tried to avoid conflict with Indians."
    D) "It is easy to defeat the Indians because they do not fight with honor or bravery."

9. Which statement about the Sand Creek Massacre is NOT true?
    A) The brutal attack included the killing of women and children.
    B) The fighting began when Indians attacked a mining town.
    C) Many white Easterners expressed outrage over the killings.
    D) The Cheyennes were killed despite their avocation of peace.

10. The leader of the Sand Creek Massacre, John Chivington, was
    A) a veteran hero of the Battle of Gettysburg.
    B) sent by President Lincoln to negotiate with the Sioux.
    C) an advocate of assimilation and coexistence.
    D) a Methodist minister.

11. At the Battle of One Hundred Slain,
    A) the Sioux routed a detachment that was sent to defeat them.
    B) the Cheyenne were defeated for the final time.
    C) the Apaches were defeated, but Geronimo escaped.
    D) the forces led by General Custer were annihilated.

12. The Sioux were finally defeated
    A) after their defeat at the Battle of Little Big Horn.
    B) due to their inexperience in battle situations.
    C) because it was difficult for them to sustain their traditional Indian economy.
    D) as a result Crazy Horse's failed offensive at the Battle of Rosebud.

13. It took 5,000 U.S. troops to capture 36 Apaches led by
    A) Sitting Bull.
    B) Geronimo.
    C) Crazy Horse.
    D) Black Kettle.

14. White reformers on the Board of Indian Commissioners believed that
    A) Indians should be left to live in their traditional ways.
    B) Indians should not be taught to speak English.
    C) Indians should be assimilated by teaching them to be Christians.
    D) Indians should never have to accept the concepts of capitalism.

15. What happened at Wounded Knee, South Dakota in 1890?
    A) The Dawes Act was signed by representatives of the Sioux.
    B) At least 200 Sioux men, women, and children were slaughtered.
    C) Geronimo was captured after eluding the army for two years.
    D) Red Cloud addressed his tribe for the final time.

16. Effects of the Dawes Act included
    A) more Indian land being owned by whites.
    B) the widespread conversion of Indians to Christianity.
    C) a sharing of natural resources between whites and Indians.
    D) an immediate attack, by the Sioux, against the U.S. army.

17. The first large gold rush occurred in
    A) the northern mountains of California.
    B) the mountains of Colorado.
    C) the desert plains of Arizona.
    D) northwestern Oregon.

18. All of the following statements are true about typical mining towns EXCEPT
    A) populations were overwhelmingly male.
    B) saloons were very prevalent among local businesses.
    C) personal violence was less common than collective acts of violence.
    D) as towns developed, local agriculture and transportation decreased.

19. Which statement about prostitutes in mining towns is NOT true?
    A) Many prostitutes came from broken homes.
    B) As men came to control vice, many prostitutes suffered alcoholism and
       violence.
    C) Most prostitutes were able to save enough to buy small homes or businesses.
    D) Many women chose prostitution because economic options were limited for
       them.

20. In *Roughing It*, Mark Twain wrote that men became influential in mining towns by selling

        A) governmental positions.

        B) guns.

        C) whiskey.

        D) pardons for cattle-rustling.

21. What was significant about the town of Bodie, California, between 1877 and 1883?

        A) It experienced twenty-nine killings brought on by mine disputes.

        B) More men became wealthy than in any other mining town.

        C) Indians won battles with whites and recaptured their land.

        D) Citizenship was restricted to white Protestants.

22. Which group suffered from the most prejudice in mining towns?

        A) Native-born whites

        B) Irish-Americans

        C) Chinese-Americans

        D) German-Americans

23. Mining eventually became a corporate operation because

        A) individual miners left the region because of conflict with Indians.

        B) Indians sold their native lands to mining capitalists.

        C) massive capital investment in equipment was conducive to financial success.

        D) ethnic disputes destroyed unity in old mining towns.

24. The mining industry entered a new era of commercial success with the mining of

        A) coal.

        B) quartz.

        C) gypsum.

        D) anthracite.

25. The _____ was an area Texans used to drive their cattle through Indian territory northward to Abilene.

        A) Trail of Tears

        B) Chisholm Trail

        C) Longhorns

        D) None of the above

When?

1. What is the correct order of events?

        A) Gold found in Colorado, Sand Creek Massacre, Battle of Little Big Horn

        B) Sand Creek Massacre, gold found in Colorado, Battle of Little Big Horn

        C) Sand Creek Massacre, Battle of Little Big Horn, gold found in Colorado

        D) Battle of Little Big Horn, gold found in Colorado, Sand Creek Massacre

2. Which headline would have appeared in 1890?
    A) "Invention of Barbed Wire Will Revolutionize Farming on the Great Plains."
    B) "Civil-War General Custer Killed by Sioux Attack."
    C) "Rail Line Stretches to Pacific Coast!"
    D) "Ghost Dance Ended as Militia Executes Sioux."

3. Which event happened first?
    A) "Exodusters" migrated to Kansas
    B) Dawes Act was passed
    C) Fort Laramie Treaty was signed
    D) Homestead Act was passed

4. Which event happened last?
    A) gold discovered in Idaho
    B) the Battle of Little Big Horn
    C) the massacre at Wounded Knee, South Dakota
    D) transcontinental railroad completed

5. "Exoduster" towns of blacks were established in Kansas and Nebraska in the
    A) 1860s.
    B) 1870s.
    C) 1880s.
    D) 1890s.

Where?

Matching

Match the place with the state in which it was located.

Promontory Point	South Dakota
Wounded Knee	Texas
Chisholm Trail	Utah
Bozeman Trail	Montana
Coeur d'Alene	Idaho

Map Skills

Use Map 19-1 from your text to answer the following questions.

1. Name the railroad that ran through Texas.

2. What territory did the Chisholm Trail run through?

3. What areas in Nevada yielded silver?

4. The Northern Pacific railroad ran through which states?

5. Where was the largest discovery of Gold in South Dakota?

How and Why?

1. What technological advances changed farming and mining in the West?

2. What unique challenges faced white settlers on the Great Plains?

3. In what ways did the Dawes Act aid and/or harm Indians?

4. What was *Americanization*? How did it attempt to change the lives of the Indians? In your opinion, was it successful or not?

5. How was the nature of the Cattle Kingdom changed by labor and environmental conditions?

6. What were the major cultural differences that led to conflicts between whites and Indians on the Great Plains? Describe specific examples of these conflicts. Do you feel that these conflicts could have been avoided? Why or why not?

7. What role did the mining industry play in migration to the West? What social trends and conflicts emerged as result of this expansion of mining into the West?

8. Compare and contrast the lives of women in the working class of the industrial Northeast with the lives of pioneer women of the Great Plains. If you had to choose, which life would you have preferred?

9. How did railroads shape the settlement and development of the West? Give examples of the positive and negative effects of the rail lines spreading from coast to coast.

10. Analyze the cultural confrontations and class conflicts that developed as the railroad industry, Cattle Kingdom, and mining industry grew.

Chapter 20
Politics and Government, 1877-1900

Practice Test

1. Which statement about presidential elections in the period 1876-1900 is true?
   A) Elections received little interest in small towns of the Midwest.
   B) Many men began to call for women's suffrage so that activism would increase.
   C) New immigrants rarely voted because they felt alienated from the process.
   D) Overall voter turnout was far greater than ever achieved after that period.

2. A major difference between elections in the late 1800s and today's elections is
   A) ethnic minorities of the North rarely voted in the late 1800s.
   B) many states had much more effective registration laws in the late 1800s.
   C) partisan aspects of elections were not a major factor in the late 1800s.
   D) a lack of privacy when voting was far more prevalent in the late 1800s.

3. New York, New Jersey, Ohio, and Indiana were key states in national elections because
   A) those states possessed 75% of the nation's electoral votes.
   B) the Republican Party garnered 80% of the votes in those states.
   C) those states were evenly contested between the Democrats and Republicans.
   D) all members of the Supreme Court came from one of those four states.

4. The Democratic Party of the late 1800s was strongest
   A) in the South where they were seen as the defender of traditions.
   B) with African-Americans loyal to the party's role as the liberator of ex-slaves.
   C) in the North among old-stock Americans.
   D) with ethnic immigrants of the North from nations such as Germany and Sweden.

5. Republicans of the late 1800's identified their party with all of the following images EXCEPT
   A) the promotion of limited government.
   B) being the party of national unity.
   C) supporting measures that would encourage cultural uniformity.
   D) feeling threatened by the huge increase in Catholic immigrants.

6. The Democrats of the late 1800s portrayed themselves as the party of
   A) the industrial Northeast.
   B) aggressive national unity.
   C) limited government and personal liberties.
   D) protective tariffs and advocacy of Indian rights.

7. The _____ supported abolition of alcohol and introduced reform ideas that are still to this day in existence.
    A) Greenback Party
    B) Progressive Party
    C) Prohibition Party
    D) Populist Party

8. The Greenback Party of the 1870s
    A) called for labor reform and democratization of the economy.
    B) represented the laissez-faire philosophy of conservative industrialists.
    C) played upon people's dissatisfaction with the Populist Party.
    D) failed to attract supporters across regional lines.

9. The Mugwumps believed that
    A) the property of the Catholic Church should be taxed.
    B) protective tariffs would revive the economy.
    C) the government should not interfere with the national economy.
    D) strict government regulation should be used to help ailing farmers.

10. The word *suffrage* is synonymous with the right to
    A) strike.
    B) survive.
    C) free expression.
    D) vote.

11. By the mid-1890s, female reformers had succeeded in
    A) getting the federal government to outlaw child labor.
    B) gaining the right to vote for women in some western states.
    C) electing several women to the U.S. Senate.
    D) convincing the American Federation of Labor to accept women as members.

12. The leader of the Women's Christian Temperance union argued that
    A) school prayer should be a vital aspect of public education.
    B) alcohol abuse was a result of poverty and social disorder.
    C) violent crime against women was not a serious social problem.
    D) the government should control the production of alcohol and tobacco.

13. The presidents in the era of 1877-1897 were known for
    A) their assertive support of labor.
    B) liberal views regarding social reform.
    C) their weak use of presidential powers.
    D) sponsoring many legislative actions.

14. The presidential duties of the late 1800s were often consumed by
    A) responsibilities regarding office-seekers and other administrative duties.
    B) promoting a more active role of the president in legislative matters.
    C) trying to calm animosities between the two major political parties.
    D) the overwhelming responsibility of personally controlling the federal bureaucracy.

15. Congress did all of the following EXCEPT
    A) debated public issues.
    B) oversaw the budget.
    C) controlled legislation.
    D) gladly accepted advice from the president.

16. The most accurate description of the *spoils system* is
    A) using the powers of state government to bypass federal laws.
    B) the promotion of third-party candidates as voices of reform.
    C) creating voting blocs based on ethnic and religious ties.
    D) awarding patronage jobs based on party activism and loyalty.

17. Rutherford B. Hayes showed he had some sympathy for civil service reform when he
    A) created the Civil Service Commission.
    B) embraced the platform of the Mugwumps.
    C) fired Chester A. Arthur after charges of corruption.
    D) refused to appoint people who had aided his campaign.

18. The Pendleton Civil Service Act began the move toward
    A) attaining the right to a secret ballot.
    B) separating partisan politics from attaining government jobs.
    C) regulating government jobs under the jurisdiction of Congressional leaders.
    D) deemphasizing skill as a qualification for government jobs.

19. Advocates of high protective tariffs asserted all of the following ideas EXCEPT
    A) tariffs would protect the domestic market.
    B) tariffs were needed to restrict competition.
    C) tariffs would promote industrial growth.
    D) tariffs were needed as a valuable source of revenue.

20. The McKinley Tariff Act
    A) deemphasized the prominence of tariffs in the American economy.
    B) raised tariffs to unprecedented levels.
    C) sought to ease the grievances expressed by farmers of the West and South.
    D) received the support of Grover Cleveland.

21. The Interstate Commerce Commission was
    A) unsuccessful in enforcing the public's call for regulating the railroad industry.
    B) supported by the big-business interests of the Republican Party.
    C) a consistent advocate of deregulating federal farming policies.
    D) created to give more power to the states in regulating commerce.

22. The Sherman Antitrust Act
    A) strengthened the collective-bargaining rights of labor.
    B) broke up the monopoly of Standard Oil Corporation.
    C) was used by Grover Cleveland's attorney general to prosecute industrialists.
    D) failed to stop the unfettered growth of large corporations.

23. Bankers' concept of a *sound money* policy favored
    A) a switch toward a silver-backed currency.
    B) implementation of the sub-treasury plan.
    C) extending the flow of currency in the South.
    D) limiting the money supply to maintain property values.

24. In which part of the country were railroad freight rates the highest?
    A) North and East
    B) South and West
    C) North and West
    D) East and South

25. The Farmers' Alliance included all of the following traits EXCEPT:
    A) restricted its membership to men of the "producing class."
    B) restricted its membership to men and women of the "producing class."
    C) was a grassroots movement.
    D) looked to bring about economic and political reform.

When?

Directions- Fill in the letter of the decade in which each historical event occurred.

A= 1870s   B= 1880s   C= 1890s

1. _____ William McKinley is elected to the first of two consecutive presidential terms.

2. _____ The Farmers Alliance is formed as a voice of the farmers in the West and South.

3. _____ The Women's Christian Temperance Union is organized.

4. _____ Congress passes the Interstate Commerce Act.

5. _____ Coxey's Army marches on Washington to protest the government's inaction regarding the needs of common people.

6. _____ The Populist Party experiences great popularity in the South and West.

7. _____ A harsh and lengthy depression worsened conditions for not only farmers, but other Americans as well.

Where?

Matching

Match the figure with his home state.

James Garfield	New York
William McKinley	Ohio
Benjamin Harrison	Indiana
Jacob Coxey	Delaware
Richard Croker	Massachusetts

Map Skills

Use Map 20-2 from your text to answer and label the following questions.

1. William Jennings Bryan carried what part of the country?

2. Nonvoting territories were located in what area of the country?

3. William McKinley won by how many popular votes over Bryan and the minor parties?

4. Did the minor parties play an important role in the outcome of this election?

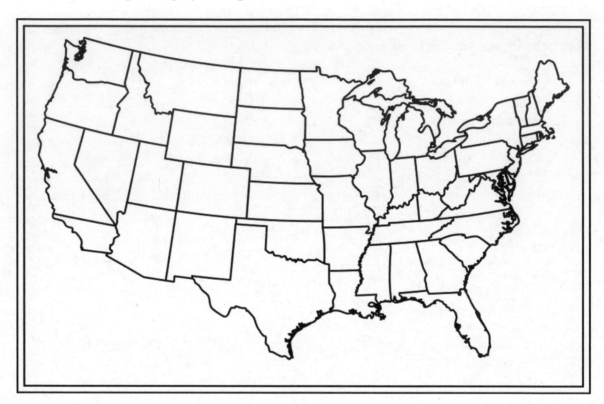

How and Why?

1. What factors determined the party affiliation of American voters in the period 1876-1900?

2. What factors limited the powers of the presidency in the last quarter of the nineteenth century?

3. In what ways did the court system support the goals and philosophies of big industry?

4. Compare and contrast the support for sound money policies versus support for the free silver movement.

5. How did the depression of the mid-1890s enhance the political position of the Republican Party?

6. Describe and evaluate the reasons for the rapid rise and fall of the Populist Party. What strengths and weaknesses were exhibited by the party?

7. What were the social and institutional factors that shaped the disorderly nature of elections in the late nineteenth century?

8. What evidence reveals that women were now becoming leaders in many of the nation's most influential reform movements?

9. Analyze the appeal of the Omaha Platform to people who felt that industrialism was too dominant in the economic and social foundation of the United States.

10. Some historians have called the presidential election of 1896 "the nation's first 'modern' election." Evaluate the validity of this statement by analyzing the issues, conflicts, and campaign tactics of that election.

Chapter 21
The Progressive Era, 1900-1917

Practice Test

1. The "progressive movement" was driven by
   A) the ideas of Eugene Debs.
   B) a general belief that moderate reforms were needed to help end social disorder.
   C) the contention that individualism, and not government help, could solve social ills.
   D) the leadership of the Populist Party.

2. All of the following are true about working conditions in the early 1900s EXCEPT:
   A) America consistently led the world in industrial accidents and deaths on the job.
   B) industrialists refused to resort to the subdivision of labor.
   C) wages were so low that most industrial workers made less than a living wage.
   D) workers were plagued by unsanitary, dangerous working conditions.

3. The immigrants known as *new immigrants* included all of the following groups EXCEPT
   A) Russian Jews.
   B) Italians.
   C) Poles.
   D) Irish Protestants.

4. Americans of "Old Stock" sometimes disliked new immigrants because
   A) they felt that the immigrants were taking desirable, middle-class jobs.
   B) they believed the presence of immigrants hurt moves toward improving worker safety.
   C) they viewed the mostly Catholic and Jewish immigrants as threats to social stability.
   D) they objected to the Republican Party's recruiting of immigrant voters.

5. The settlement house movement was established to
   A) improve conditions for new immigrants.
   B) promote reformist candidates for political office.
   C) act as a political lobby group for the rights of new Americans.
   D) monitor businesses and ensure decent working conditions.

6. Leaders of the Social Gospel movement sought to
    A) establish parochial schools in urban neighborhoods.
    B) introduce religious ethics to industrial relations.
    C) combine religion with laissez-faire philosophies.
    D) back Socialist candidates for national office.

7. Proponents of the Social Gospel believed in all of the following ideas EXCEPT
    A) empathizing with the plight of the working poor.
    B) emphasizing a literal interpretation of the Old Testament.
    C) advocating a wider tolerance of different religious faiths.
    D) promoting the role of Christianity in addressing social problems.

8. The main goal of the muckrakers was to
    A) support socialistic policies in the U.S. Congress.
    B) raise the public's awareness of social problems.
    C) ruin the reputations of presidential candidates.
    D) end the legality of alcohol consumption.

9. Which work of literature was NOT authored by a muckraker?
    A) *The Jungle*
    B) *The Octopus*
    C) *The Shame of the Cities*
    D) *Christianity and the Social Crisis*

10. The Social Gospel movement was not popular with which religious group?
    A) Episcopalians
    B) Catholics
    C) Congregationalists
    D) Methodists

11. Theodore Roosevelt's reform philosophy was closest to that of
    A) muckraking journalists.
    B) the Knights of Labor.
    C) the Gospel of Efficiency.
    D) the Social Gospel Movement.

12. Frederick Taylor's *scientific management* emphasized all of the following ideas EXCEPT
    A) providing more autonomy for the factory laborer.
    B) speeding up the production process.
    C) increasing the mechanization of factories.
    D) assigning simple, repetitive tasks to workers.

13. Wobblies were members of which group?
    A) A.F.L.
    B) Amalgamated Clothing Workers
    C) Industrial Workers of the World
    D) None of the above

14. The members of the Ladies Garment Workers Union and the Amalgamated Clothing Workers were predominantly Jewish and _____.
    A) Japanese
    B) Italian
    C) German
    D) Mexican

15. Which of the following statements about women in the early 1900s is NOT true?
    A) More women than before were working outside the home.
    B) Women began to organize their own labor unions.
    C) Less working women were choosing to get married.
    D) Women's clubs were becoming seedbeds of many reform movements.

16. The Feminist Alliance formed in response to the
    A) Triangle Shirtwaist fire.
    B) firing of female New York teachers when they married.
    C) the practice of only allowing skilled women laborers in the A.F.L.
    D) Homestead Steel strike.

17. An accomplishment of the Women's Trade Union League was that it
    A) convinced Congress to end child labor.
    B) united working-class and middle-class women in one group.
    C) provided an outlet of protest without resorting to strikes.
    D) merged with the American Federation of Labor.

18. Most American socialists did NOT advocate
    A) the creation of a stronger central government.
    B) public ownership of railroads and utilities.
    C) economic change accomplished through political action.
    D) a worldwide revolution by the working class.

19. Which Party did Eugene Debs help to organize?
    A) Reformist
    B) Progressive
    C) Socialist
    D) Communist

20. All of the following groups or people opposed progressive social reforms EXCEPT
    A) Billy Sunday.
    B) Protestant fundamentalists.
    C) supporters of the Social Gospel Movement.
    D) John D. Rockefeller.

21. Who founded the National Housing Association in 1910?
    A) Lincoln Steffens
    B) Lawrence Veiller
    C) Jane Addams
    D) Frederick Taylor

22. A peak of anti-union violence occurred when
    A) police broke up a memorial parade for workers killed in the Triangle Shirtwaist fire.
    B) supporters of Eugene Debs marched to Washington D.C.
    C) Robert La Follette was nominated for president.
    D) John D. Rockefeller ordered that striking miners, and their families, be shot.

23. Most settlement houses were staffed by
    A) industrial laborers during off-hours.
    B) middle-class women.
    C) foreign-born socialists.
    D) union organizers.

24. A leader of the housing reform movement and a worker at University Settlement was
    A) Billy Sunday.
    B) Charles Sheldon.
    C) Walter Rauschenbush.
    D) Lawrence Veiller.

25. Reformers who focused on ending child labor faced resistance from big business and
    A) the American Federation of Labor.
    B) leaders of the settlement-house movement.
    C) believers in the Social Gospel Movement.
    D) some poor parents who needed the extra income.

When?

Directions- Fill in the letter of the president who was in office when each reform act was passed by Congress.

A= Theodore Roosevelt   B= William Howard Taft   C= Woodrow Wilson

1. _____ Federal Trade Commission is established.

2. _____ Hepburn Act strengthens the Interstate Commerce Commission.

3. _____ Constitutional Amendment initiates a national income tax.

4. _____ Mann-Elkins act extends authority of I.C.C. over telephone and telegraph companies.

5. _____ Keating-Owen Act prohibits interstate shipment of products made by child labor.

6. _____ The National Farmers Union was formed.

7. _____ The National Conservation Commission is established.

8. _____ The Nineteenth Amendment was ratified.

9. _____ The Federal Reserve Act created 12 regional Federal Reserve banks.

10. _____ The Underwood-Simmons Tariff Act provided the first substantial reduction in duties since before the Civil War.

Where?

Matching

Match the figures with their home states.

Frances Kellor	Mississippi
Samuel Jones	New York
Hoke Smith	Ohio
Washington Gladden	Georgia
Robert La Follette	Wisconsin

Map Skills

Use Map 21-1 from your text to answer and label the following questions

1. When did the National Forest system begin?

2. Which National Park is the furthest north on the east coast?

3. Which National Park was established first in Alaska?

4. Organ Pipe Cactus National Park is in what state?

5. Which park was established first?

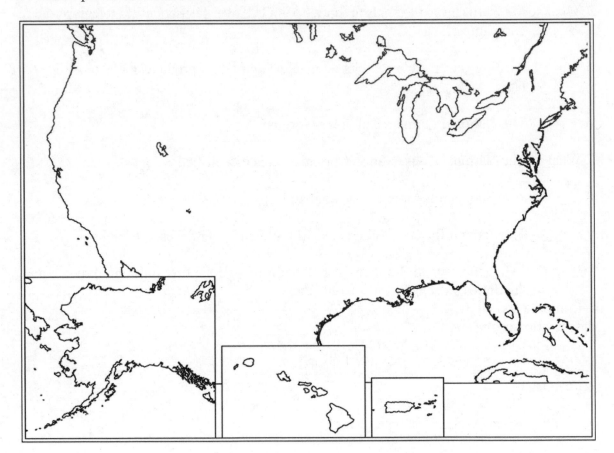

How and Why?

1. What characteristics defined the philosophy of Americans who fell under the general category of "progressives"?

2. What social elements were combined behind the move to pass prohibition legislation?

3. What were examples of reform in city and rural areas?

4. Compare and contrast the ideas of those Americans who believed in either conservation or preservation.

5. What amendments to the Constitution were passed in the period 1910-1920?

6. Compare and contrast the ideas of reform expressed by two of the three following presidents:

Theodore Roosevelt, William Howard Taft, and Woodrow Wilson.

7. Some historians feel that Theodore Roosevelt was the "first modern president" of the twentieth century. What evidence supports this claim? In what ways do you feel this is true or untrue?

8. In what ways did social reform and social control often intermingle in the Progressive Era? Which impulse was more prevalent in the period 1905-1918?

9. How did the role of women change during the Progressive Era? What effect did this have on the progress of progressivism?

10. What views of reform were expressed by labor, blacks, and the Socialist Party? What effect did their views have on the nature of reform?

Chapter 22
Creating an Empire, 1865-1917

Practice Test

1. Major outcomes of the Spanish-American War included all of the following EXCEPT
    A) reluctance of the government to get involved in other foreign conflicts.
    B) the emergence of the nation's status as a world power.
    C) the establishment of an extensive American empire.
    D) the beginning of a new period of opportunity and problems in foreign policy.

2. Rationales for imperialism in the era 1890-1910 included all of the following ideas EXCEPT
    A) American ideas and institutions were superior to those of inferior nations.
    B) the spread of Christianity would help lesser nations develop morally.
    C) American prosperity now depended on larger access to foreign markets and resources.
    D) the United States needed a vast buffer zone to offset communist expansionism.

3. Which statement would most likely have been said by a believer in Social Darwinism who was addressing the issue of imperialism?
    A) "The very laws of nature reveal that national identity is not related to cultural worth."
    B) "We must isolate ourselves from the uncivilized cultures of distant lands."
    C) "American expansionism should most logically be restricted to North America."
    D) "We must promote the superiority of our culture in an effort to ensure world stability."

4. Mahan's program was mainly supported by the republicans from the
    A) Southwest.
    B) West.
    C) Southeast.
    D) Northeast.

5. American imperialists often rationalized actions by
    A) pointing out that the United States had to overcome a heritage of a weak military.
    B) claiming western European nations were weak because they did not annex territory.
    C) expressing the opinion people of Anglo-Saxon descent were from a superior culture.
    D) refusing to admit to the economic benefits that could be gained from imperial colonies.

6. *Mahanism* emphasized
    A) the spread of Christianity to remote nations.
    B) opposition to the new imperialism of the United States.
    C) the importance of the navy in imperial expansion.
    D) the equality of people who lived in imperial territories.

7. One reason for the widespread support for a larger navy was
    A) its role in providing jobs for the nation's unemployed men
    B) many people believed that an army was no longer a necessity.
    C) the belief that the navy could effectively block further immigration.
    D) its use to expand and protect America's international trade.

8. The primary goal of the American government's imperialistic policies was
    A) religious conversion.
    B) colonial conquest.
    C) military attacks.
    D) economic expansion.

9. Economic conditions that fueled support for foreign trade included
    A) a decrease in the number of wage earners.
    B) the seemingly unlimited prosperity of the years 1888-1895.
    C) a huge increase in the amount of manufactured goods produced in America.
    D) the nation's decision to use a silver-backed currency.

10. Who purchased Alaska?
    A) Hay
    B) Jay
    C) Seward
    D) Blaine

11. The first international American conference called for
    A) stronger foreign relations with Canada.
    B) reduce trade barriers.
    C) reduce foreign imports.
    D) provided government inertest in private affairs.

12. The American government used all of the following methods to take control of Hawaii EXCEPT
    A) using economic embargo by closing U.S. markets to sugar producers.
    B) endorsing a Hawaiian constitution that gave power to wealthy white residents.
    C) enlisting the help of Great Britain and France in establishing imperial control.
    D) sending the Marines to support a move to overthrow Queen Liliuokalani.

13. The effort to annex Hawaii in 1893 foreshadowed
    A) a 20-year period of uninterrupted warfare between the U.S. and Hawaiians.
    B) the aggressive imperialistic policies of Grover Cleveland.
    C) the differences between Republicans and Democrats regarding imperialism.
    D) America's reliance on France to take the lead in determining foreign policy.

14. One effect of the border dispute between Britain and Venezuela over British Guiana was
    A) America's decision to abandon the ideas of the Monroe Doctrine.
    B) a brief straining of relations between the U.S. and Britain.
    C) the emergence of consistent U.S. support for Britain in Latin America.
    D) the onset of an economic depression in the Western Hemisphere.

15. Which statement best describes the duality of causes for American intervention in Cuba?
    A) Americans were motivated by commercial concerns and their support for freedom.
    B) Americans wished to stop British expansionism and secure markets in the Pacific.
    C) The American government wanted to stop Cuban exports and revolutionary ideology.
    D) Republicans wanted to defy President Cleveland and open markets in the Caribbean.

16. Before the Spanish-American War, the *yellow press*
    A) used sensationalism to stir up war fever.
    B) wrote editorials that criticized American imperialism.
    C) refused to write about foreign affairs.
    D) endorsed a policy of isolationism.

17. Populists supported intervention in Cuba because
    A) they felt taking this position would aid their presidential candidate.
    B) the Republican Party overwhelmingly opposed intervention.
    C) they sympathized with the Cubans' quest for freedom.
    D) the party's platform called for deregulation of trade with Cuba.

18. McKinley wanted to acquire the Philippines because of the following EXCEPT:
    A) He needed to strengthen American political position in East Asia.
    B) He felt Filipinos not able to rule themselves.
    C) He feared Germany or Japan might seize Philippines if the United States did not.
    D) He was willing to concede Puerto Rico and Guam.

19. Commodore George Dewey led the Americans to victory
    A) at San Juan Hill.
    B) in the Hawaiian Islands.
    C) at San Jacinto.
    D) in Manila Bay.

20. Theodore Roosevelt headed this militia in the Spanish American War
    A) the Anti-Imperialists.
    B) Rough Riders.
    C) the 10th Negro Cavalry.
    D) the 19th Marine Unit.

21. During the Spanish-American War,
    A) the Americans won a relatively easy victory.
    B) the American navy showed vulnerability.
    C) aid from France was vital to the American victory.
    D) America won despite suffering much heavier casualties than Spain.

22. As a result of the Spanish-American War,
    A) Theodore Roosevelt emerged as an anti-imperialist.
    B) William McKinley expressed the desire to acquire the Philippines.
    C) Congress voted to declare Philippine independence.
    D) William McKinley was not reelected.

23. Who was NOT opposed to the Treaty of Paris?
    A) William Jennings Bryan
    B) Andrew Carnegie
    C) Theodore Roosevelt
    D) Jane Addams

24. Similarities between the Spanish American War and Filipino War include all of the following EXCEPT
    A) the native population had been ruled by another nation before American involvement.
    B) the native population sought independence from Spain.
    C) brutal methods were used against the native population.
    D) It took the same number of soldiers to fight each war.

25. All of the following statements about the Filipino War are true EXCEPT
    A) the military imposed censorship on war news.
    B) little effort was made to distinguish between combatants and civilians.
    C) subsequent colonial rule was somewhat benign and paternalistic.
    D) fewer soldiers were used in this war than in the Spanish American War.

When?

Directions- Fill in the letter of the president with the actions taken during their terms of office.

A= William McKinley   B= Theodore Roosevelt   C= William Howard Taft
D= Woodrow Wilson

1. _____ The Spanish-American War is won by the U.S.

2. _____ Marines occupy the Dominican Republic.

3. _____ The American president attempts to aggressively become involved in the internal politics of Mexico.

4. _____ The United States purchases the Panama Canal.

5. _____ The bitter Filipino-American War begins.

6. _____ America expresses support for Japan in the Russo-Japanese War.

7. _____ The Boxer Rebellion, a nationalist uprising, is defeated in China by a multinational military force.

8. _____ American forces intervene in Nicaragua for the first time.

Where?

Matching

Match the following people with their home states.

Henry Cabot Lodge	Virginia
Queen Liliuokalani	Hawaii
George Vest	Massachusetts
John Mitchell	Missouri
Emilio Aguinaldo	Philippines

Map Skills

Use Map 22-3 to answer and label the following questions.

1. How many years elapsed from the time the US acquired the Panama Canal Zone until the canal's completion?

2. In what year did the US seize Vera Cruz?

3. Who had ownership of Guadeloupe?

4. In what year was the US naval base Guantanamo established?

5. When did Puerto Rico become a US 'possession'?

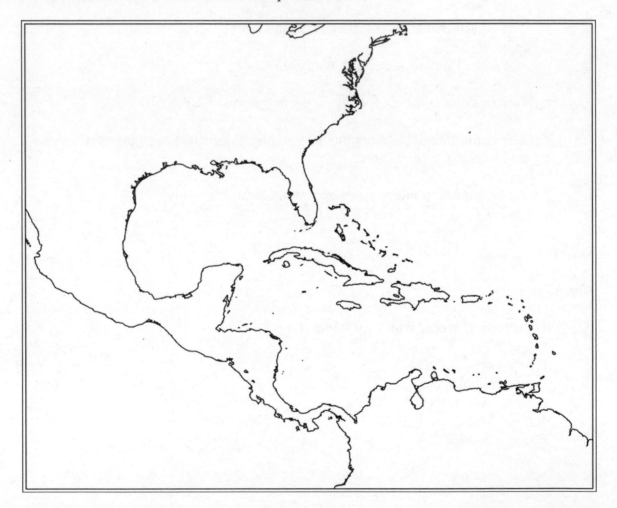

178

How and Why?

1. Describe the connection between: spheres of influence, the Open Door policy, and dollar diplomacy.

2. What were the important consequences of the American victory in the Spanish-American War?

3. What factors contributed to making the Filipino-American War a controversial, bitter, and hard-fought conflict?

4. Describe the ideas expressed by those who dissented against interventionist policies of the American government.

5. What example, to you, represented America's most aggressive use of interventionist policy in the period 1890-1918?

6. How effective were U.S. interventions in Latin America? What were the objectives and consequences? Do you tend to agree or disagree with these interventions?

7. Compare and contrast the foreign policies of two of the following four presidents: William McKinley, Theodore Roosevelt, William Howard Taft, and Woodrow Wilson.

8. In what ways was Woodrow Wilson among the most interventionist presidents in U.S. history?

9. What combination of causes led to the American involvement in the Spanish-American War? What were the key factors in producing a quick American victory?

10. How did American foreign policy combine economic, military, and political strategies? In what ways did American intervention differ from traditional European imperialism?

Chapter 23
America and the Great War, 1914-1920

Practice Test

1. In August of 1914, as war erupted in Europe, most Americans
    A) felt that America should maintain a neutral role in the conflict.
    B) believed that the U.S. government should fund England's war effort.
    C) called for direct American military involvement on the Western Front.
    D) protested against President Wilson's decision to send troops.

2. When a Serbian nationalist killed Archduke Ferdinand, it ignited an alliance system that immediately set up an ominous conflict between
    A) France and England.
    B) Russia and France.
    C) Germany and England.
    D) Russia and Germany.

3. All of the following nations belonged to the Central Powers EXCEPT
    A) Japan.
    B) Austria.
    C) Germany.
    D) Turkey.

4. Which statement does NOT characterize the first two years of the Great War?
    A) Mass slaughter occurred as new weapons of war were used.
    B) Conditions in the battle trenches caused the spread of diseases.
    C) The Germans consistently pushed the Allies back in battles.
    D) Each side dug trenches that extended from Belgium to Switzerland.

5. Who tended to sympathize with the Allies in the first years of the war?
    A) President Wilson and most of his advisers
    B) Americans feeling closer affinity to western democracy than German authoritarianism
    C) those who felt closer cultural ties with British and French culture
    D) all of the above

6. Even before direct American involvement, the U.S. was linked to the Allies' cause
    A) as a result of Russia's hostility to American trade with Britain.
    B) because of the valuable loans that banks had issued to Allied nations.
    C) due to the presence of U.S. marines on Allied warships.
    D) as a result of Germany's refusal to follow the Declaration of London.

7. The 1909 agreement, the Declaration of London, was designed to protect the rights of
    A) the British navy's presence in the Mediterranean.
    B) soldiers taken as prisoners of war.
    C) nations who were neutral in military conflicts.
    D) English citizens who lived in Turkey and Bulgaria.

8. Germany resorted to submarine warfare
    A) after U.S. merchant marine ships had fired upon German destroyers.
    B) to illustrate its technological superiority over the Allies.
    C) as a way of diverting attention from its military defeats on the Western Front.
    D) in its effort to break England's naval blockade on trade with the Central
       Powers.

9. All of the following statements about the sinking of the *Lusitania* are true EXCEPT
    A) over 100 Americans were killed.
    B) a German submarine sunk the British passenger liner.
    C) it is now known that the ship was carrying arms.
    D) it led to the immediate American involvement in the Great War.

10. President Wilson's response to the sinking of the *Lusitania*
    A) was supported by his secretary of state, William Jennings Bryan.
    B) led to his support for the Gore-McLemore resolutions.
    C) included the president's assertive demand that Germany end its submarine
       warfare.
    D) reflected the nation's rigid commitment to maintain neutrality at all costs.

11. A policy of war *preparedness* was advocated by
    A) Jane Addams.
    B) Theodore Roosevelt.
    C) William Jennings Bryan.
    D) the Socialist Party.

12. The *Sussex* Pledge required that both Britain and what other country adhere to the rules of international law universally recognized before the war?
    A) Italy
    B) Japan
    C) Germany
    D) Russia

13. One effect of German submarine warfare was
    A) Americans became convinced that the Allies had no chance of winning the
       war.
    B) many Americans felt that England should surrender.
    C) the Republican Party intensified its belief in neutrality.
    D) President Wilson called for expansion of the armed forces.

14. What was ironic about Wilson's successful campaign slogan, "He Kept Us Out of War"?

        A) Republicans were more isolationist than most Democrats.

        B) Wilson disliked the slogan's sentiment, but exploited its political popularity.

        C) The slogan was created by Theodore Roosevelt for use by Wilson's. opponent.

        D) Americans did not realize troops had already been secretly sent to the Western Front.

15. In winning the election of 1916, Woodrow Wilson benefited from

        A) the belief of many voters that the Republicans were a "war party."

        B) the endorsement of Theodore Roosevelt.

        C) strong support in the Midwest.

        D) the unimportance of the war as a campaign issue.

16. In January 1917, President Wilson outlined a "new world order" in which

        A) self-determination would be the foundation of world relations.

        B) the United States would act as mediator of all European conflicts.

        C) freedom the seas should be reevaluated as a vital American policy.

        D) the League of Nations should be replaced by the United Nations.

17. In the Zimmerman Note, Germany promised

        A) that Mexico could regain lost territory in America if it joined the Central Powers.

        B) to refrain from submarine warfare, but then proceeded to sink several American ships.

        C) negotiate for peace with England, but not with France or Russia.

        D) to follow all statutes of the antipiracy law of 1819.

18. What happened only two weeks before America's declaration of war against Germany?

        A) President Wilson was renominated for a second term.

        B) American citizens were killed when the *Lusitania* was sunk.

        C) The War Industries Board was approved by Congress.

        D) German submarines sank four American freighters.

19. Which agency increased agricultural production and supervised food distribution?

        A) Railroad Administration

        B) National War Labor Board

        C) Food Administration

        D) Committee on Public Information

20. The War Industries Board was established to organize all of the following EXCEPT
   A) the coordination of military purchasing.
   B) the criteria for drafting soldiers.
   C) allocating scarce materials and standardizing production.
   D) establishing industrial priorities during the war.

21. The head of the War Industries Board was
   A) Bernard Baruch.
   B) Henry Cabot Lodge.
   C) Robert La Follette.
   D) Claude Kitchen.

22. The Railroad administration was led by
   A) Bernard Baruch.
   B) Woodrow Wilson.
   C) William McAdoo.
   D) Claude Kitchin.

23. The Food Administration was led by
   A) Woodrow Wilson.
   B) Herbert Hoover.
   C) Hiram Johnson.
   D) Wilham McAdoo.

24. The National War Labor Board did all of the following EXCEPT
   A) improve working conditions.
   B) garner higher wages.
   C) stipulate an 8-hour workday.
   D) decrease wages.

25. It was estimated that _____ women had replaced men in industry during the war?
   A) 50,000
   B) 75,000
   C) 250,000
   D) 1,000,000

When?

1. Which event happened first?
   A) President Wilson was reelected.
   B) The Zimmerman Note was intercepted.
   C) The *Lusitania* was sunk.
   D) American troops were sent to the Western Front.

2. Which headline would have appeared in 1920?

A) "Beaten Germans Announce Surrender of Central Powers"
B) "Harding New President After Landslide Victory"
C) "Debs Jailed for Speaking Out Against Government"
D) "Hoover Named Chief of Food Administration"

3. Which event happened last?
  A) Women were given the right to vote in a Constitutional amendment.
  B) President Wilson announced his Fourteen Points.
  C) Congress passed the Espionage Act.
  D) World War broke out in Europe.

4. When was the suffrage amendment ratified?
  A) 1917
  B) 1918
  C) 1919
  D) 1920

5. Which event did NOT happen in 1917?
  A) U.S. declared war on Germany.
  B) Espionage Act was passed.
  C) Bolshevik Revolution occurred in Russia.
  D) Germany began submarine warfare.

Where?

Matching

Match the following figures of World War I with the country with which they are associated.

Kaiser Wilhelm II	Austria Hungary
Arthus Zimmermann	Germany
Archduke Franz Ferdinand	France
Joseph Joffre	Switzerland
V. I. Lenin	Russia

Map Skills

Use Map 23-2 from your text to answer and label the following questions.

1. What were the three neutral nations?

2. Name the farthest point north the Germans reached.

3. When was the earliest allied victory?

4. When was the latest allied victory (excluding the Armistice)?

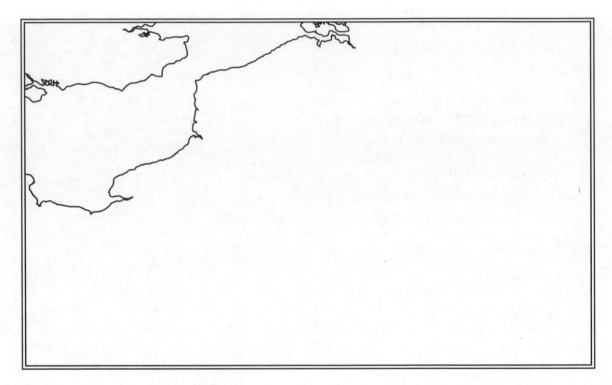

How and Why?

1. Describe the opposing views that existed regarding *preparedness*.

2. In what ways was the "neutrality" of the United States in World War I misleading?

3. At the Paris Peace Conference, what major differences of opinion existed between Woodrow Wilson, Georges Clemenceau, and Lloyd George?

4. What were the causes of a downturn in the labor movement after 1919?

5. Discuss how the lives of African Americans changed during the war.

6. Analyze American foreign policy regarding World War I in the period 1914-April, 1917. What do you feel were the main causes of America's eventual involvement in the war?

7. What role did government propaganda play in its attempt to rally Americans behind the war effort? What examples reveal the level of aggression used against those who were suspected of disloyalty?

8. Discuss the arguments for and against American ratification of the Treaty of Versailles. If you lived in that era, would you have supported ratification? Why or why not?

9. Describe the amazing range of success and failure experienced by Woodrow Wilson in the period 1912-1920.

10. What were the consequences and long-range effects of the Committee of Public Information, the Food Administration, and the War Industries Board?

Chapter 24
Toward a Modern America, The 1920s

Practice Test

1. Which text by Upton Sinclair portrayed a dramatic account of industrial America?
   A) *The Jungle*
   B) *The Flivver King*
   C) *How the Other Half Lives*
   D) *none of the above*

2. In the 1920s, Europeans used the term *Fordize* as a synonym for
   A) mechanized.
   B) imperialism.
   C) Americanize.
   D) craft union.

3. By the 1920s, workers in Henry Ford's automobile industry
   A) experienced a return to the days of labor controlled by artisanship.
   B) enjoyed the company's eclectic tolerance of ethnic diversity.
   C) were encouraged to unionize in order to form a labor and management consensus.
   D) worked in a solemn atmosphere that emphasized making money over. individuality.

4. Which statement about industry in the 1920s is NOT true?
   A) Mass production spread quickly in American industry.
   B) Businesses rejected any implementation of Taylor's scientific management.
   C) Standardized parts helped increase productivity and efficiency.
   D) Productivity in the automobile industry increased constantly.

5. Effects of the automobile industry's growth included all of the following EXCEPT
   A) boosting the petroleum and oil industries.
   B) employing one of every fourteen manufacturing workers.
   C) reducing the use of assembly-line production.
   D) spurring large increases in building residential homes.

6. DuPont emerged as a powerful corporation in the
   A) chemical industry.
   B) steel industry.
   C) movie industry.
   D) housing construction industry.

7. Which statement about the development of the radio industry is NOT true?
    A) It was not until the 1930s that radio experienced a large boom in popularity.
    B) The Federal Communications Commission was created to organize radio wave bands.
    C) Several corporations quickly rose as dominant powers in the industry.
    D) There were 732 stations by 1927.

8. A major industrial trend of the 1920s was
    A) the emergence of more competition within major industries.
    B) the decline of open shops.
    C) the concentration of wealth in the largest firms of an industry.
    D) the strengthening of local retailers.

9. All of the following were aspects of the *open shop* campaign EXCEPT
    A) the extension of collective bargaining rights for unskilled laborers.
    B) the movement was an attempt to break union shop contracts.
    C) workers often had to sign *yellow dog* contracts that rejected unions.
    D) powerful companies refused to do business with companies who had union labor.

10. Proponents of *welfare capitalism* believed that
    A) the government should provide unemployment insurance.
    B) corporations could undercut unions by providing certain benefits.
    C) the ideas of scientific management had to be entirely rejected.
    D) the national government should be more active in programs of social reform.

11. All of the following statements about labor in the 1920s are true EXCEPT
    A) increased mechanization caused greater job insecurity.
    B) the improvement in real wages reflected falling prices.
    C) unions declined in power, but membership increased.
    D) unemployment in the "sick" industries approached 30 percent.

12. As the nation's productivity increased,
    A) a high percentage of workers experienced a decent standard of living.
    B) wages were not proportionately raised.
    C) corporate taxes were raised by Republican administrations.
    D) unemployment dropped significantly.

13. Several "sick" industries experienced all of the following problems EXCEPT
    A) shrinking demand for their goods.
    B) bitter labor-management relations.
    C) excess capacity of rail lines.
    D) high corporate taxes.

14. The textile industry coped with a drop in economic prosperity by
    A) encouraging collective bargaining.
    B) lobbying Congress for heavy federal subsidies.
    C) shifting operations to the cheap-labor South.
    D) cutting back work hours.

15. During the 1920s, American agriculture
    A) maintained its role as the main strength of the American economy.
    B) never recovered from the depression of 1921.
    C) was unable to produce a surplus of crops.
    D) moved away from sharecropping and tenant farming.

16. The Republican presidents of the 20s
    A) emphasized the importance of business interests.
    B) pursued programs that provided social reform.
    C) used their power to directly aid the ailing farm economy.
    D) won narrow victories at the polls.

17. Which statement about the Harding administration is NOT true?
    A) A great deal of corruption plagued the presidential cabinet.
    B) Andrew Mellon led the move to reduce taxes for the rich.
    C) Harding made Supreme Court appointments that favored business interests.
    D) His attorney general spoke out against the "open shop" campaign.

18. Who was Harding's Secretary of the Treasury?
    A) Herbert Hoover
    B) William Howard Taft
    C) Harry Daugherty
    D) Andrew Mellon

19. Senator George Norris of Nebraska criticized the Harding administration for
    A) being far too active in foreign affairs.
    B) giving in to the demands of labor.
    C) allowing big businesses to dominate American life.
    D) opposing protective tariffs.

20. The Teapot Dome scandal
    A) was one of many scandals that plagued the Hoover administration.
    B) involved government officials illegally leasing land to oil companies.
    C) resulted in Harding's defeat in the 1924 primaries.
    D) revealed that the government was setting up monopolies in retail food sales.

21. All of the following statements about the election of 1924 are true EXCEPT
    A) the Democrats were hopelessly divided at their nominating convention.
    B) John W. Davis emerged as a formidable opponent for Calvin Coolidge.
    C) the Republicans used big-business money to attack La Follette's progressive ideas.
    D) barely 50% of the American electorate turned out to vote.

22. The Sheppard-Towner Act
    A) required less regulation of national banks.
    B) provided federal funds for infant and maternity care.
    C) ended the shame of child labor.
    D) regulated interstate commerce.

23. Which statement about living patterns in the 1920s is NOT true?
    A) African-Americans migrated in large numbers to northern cities.
    B) The single-family house became the middle-class ideal.
    C) Older industrial cities of the North continued to grow.
    D) The majority of Americans still lived in rural areas.

24. Blacks migrated to the urban North for all of the following reasons EXCEPT
    A) racial discrimination was not a part of life in the North.
    B) to escape from the constant threat of violence in the South.
    C) more job opportunities were available in the North.
    D) to escape the confining segregation of the South.

25. How many Puerto Ricans settled in New York's Spanish Harlem?
    A) 25,000
    B) 50,000
    C) 75,000
    D) 100,000

When?

1. What is the correct order of presidential succession?
    A) Harding, Hoover, Coolidge
    B) Coolidge, Harding, Hoover
    C) Harding, Coolidge, Hoover
    D) Hoover, Coolidge, Harding

2. Which event happened first?
    A) Prohibition was enacted.
    B) The Kellogg-Briand Pact was signed.
    C) Ernest Hemingway released *A Farewell to Arms*.
    D) Calvin Coolidge defeated John W. Davis.

3. Which headline would have appeared in 1927?
       A) "Nation Stunned by Sudden Death of President Harding"
       B) "Lindbergh Greeted in France by Roaring Crowd"
       C) "Women Go to the Polls for the First Time"
       D) "Addition of Sound Thrills Film Fans Across Nation"

4. Which event happened in 1928?
       A) Hoover defeated Smith in the presidential election.
       B) Baseball fans saw rookie Babe Ruth for the first time.
       C) The National Origins Act restricted immigration.
       D) Clarence Darrow defended John Scopes.

5. Which event happened last?
       A) The Scopes Trial
       B) Cecil B. De Mille released *The Ten Commandments*
       C) The Kellogg-Briand Pact was signed
       D) Eugene Debs was released from prison

Where?

Matching

Match the following organizations with the city in which they were located.

Country Club Plaza	Detroit
Royce Hailey's Pig Stand	Chicago
Yankees	Dallas
Ford Motor Company	New York
Al Capone's Army	Kansas City

Map Skills

Use Map 24-1 from your text to answer and label the following questions.

1. Which states north of Texas experienced population growth?

2. Did the New England area experience strong population growth or moderate?

3. Name three states that experienced a loss in population.

4. Which southern states saw both a strong population growth and an African-American migration?

5. The majority of the African Americans from the southeast migrated to what cities?

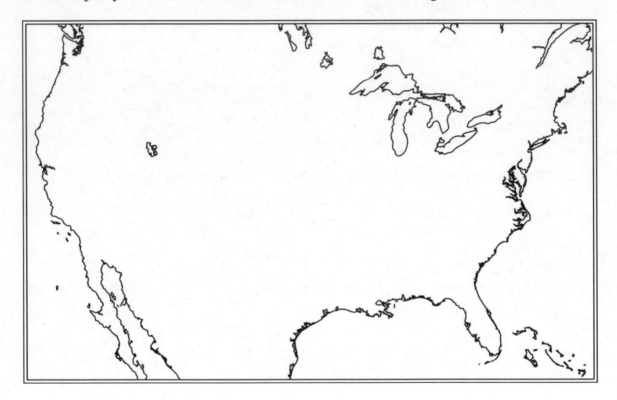

How and Why?

1. What factors characterized the "boom industries" of the 1920s?

2. In what ways did the World War I experience affect life in the 1920s?

3. What evidence reveals the close ties between big business and the Republican Party during the 1920s?

4. How did life in the South change during the 1920s?

5. Describe the beliefs and goals of nativists. Why did nativism increase in the 1920s?

6. Respond to the following statement: "The 1920s was an era in which the forces of modernization came into conflict with the forces of traditionalism."

7. Popular culture grew and prospered in the 1920s. Why was this so? Provide at lease three examples that explain why the growth occurred and how it changed people's lives in the '20s.

8. In what ways was the prosperity of the 1920s misleading? What examples led people to believe the country was beginning a period of unending prosperity? What underlying factors revealed that economic problems were just around the corner?

9. Choose three of the following groups and describe the characteristics of life for them in the 1920s: African-Americans, female reformers, young people in urban areas, fundamentalists, novelists and poets, celebrities, and union members.

10. Analyze the impact of mechanization, consumerism, advertising, and the boom in the auto industry on American life in the 1920s. Do you feel these impacts were for the betterment of American life?

Chapter 25
The Great Depression and the New Deal, 1929-1939

Practice Test

1. What occurred on "Black Tuesday"?
   A) Germany attacked Poland
   B) A stock market crash wiped all the gains of the previous year
   C) Hoover announced he would take no action regarding the faltering farm economy.
   D) U.S. steel announced a layoff of over half its workers

2. The Wall Street crash
   A) was triggered by excessive government spending.
   B) only affected middle-class Americans.
   C) marked the beginning of the depression, but did not cause it.
   D) was caused by the low level of investment in the 1920s.

3. All of the following were causes of the Great Depression EXCEPT
   A) unequal distribution of wealth.
   B) a drop in agricultural production in the mid-1920s.
   C) the dominance of oligopolies in the American economy.
   D) reckless banking and speculation unchecked by regulation.

4. In the early years of the depression,
   A) foreign markets for American goods shrank.
   B) voluntarism was rejected by the Hoover administration.
   C) unemployment had not emerged as a major problem.
   D) farmers' incomes rose dramatically.

5. The depression was prolonged when
   A) the government ordered that more exports be sold in Europe.
   B) banks voluntarily submitted to regulatory policies.
   C) the Federal Reserve Board restricted the nation's money supply.
   D) unemployment skyrocketed.

6. In the first years of the depression, personal income
   A) remained steady, but prices rose.
   B) did not emerge as a major problem area.
   C) dropped by more than half.
   D) reflected the relative strength of the industrial economy.

7. What were Hoovervilles?

    A) Squalid collections of shacks where the homeless of America's cities lived.

    B) The numerous soup kitchens that were constructed to feed the nation's hungry.

    C) Rich sections of town where wealthy Republicans lived.

    D) Suburban towns that experienced sharp downturns during the depression.

8. Which statement about women during the depression is NOT true?

    A) Women were generally less likely to be fired than men.

    B) Many of the nation's school districts refused to hire married women.

    C) Opposition to women doing "men's jobs" stiffened during the depression.

    D) Firing women usually opened up more job opportunities for men.

9. Social effects of the depression included all of the following EXCEPT

    A) lower birthrates.

    B) higher divorce rates.

    C) loss of self esteem by unemployed workers.

    D) an increase in the number of men who deserted their families.

10. During the Depression many teens

    A) left home to allow for others in the family to eat.

    B) attended school with hopes of going to college.

    C) made their own clothes.

    D) left home to escape parental authority.

11. Which statement about conditions for African-Americans during the depression is true?

    A) Unemployment rates for blacks stayed at the same high pre-depression rate.

    B) Blacks received equal treatment in receiving aid from relief programs.

    C) Blacks were generally the first workers to be fired and the last to be hired.

    D) Religious charity groups provided help for blacks.

12. During the depression, Hispanic Americans

    A) were able to move up to middle-class status.

    B) experienced little discrimination in finding work.

    C) always resisted returning to Mexico.

    D) lost many jobs due to prejudice against them.

13. Which statement best summarizes protest movements in the early years of the depression?

    A) Demonstrations were virtually nonexistent despite the awful conditions.

    B) The government passed a law that made it illegal to stage any type off protest.

    C) Protesters came from a vast range of social, political, and economic interests.

    D) Conservative Republicans dominated the ranks of those who led protest movements.

14. One of Herbert Hoover's few relief measures was creation of the
    A) Works Progress Administration.
    B) Farm Credit Act.
    C) Emergency Banking Act.
    D) Reconstruction Finance Corporation.

15. Franklin Roosevelt defeated Herbert Hoover in 1932 for all of the following reasons EXCEPT
    A) the public viewed Hoover as cold and ineffective at dealing with the depression.
    B) Roosevelt announced the specifics of his New Deal package of legislation.
    C) Hoover's public image was damaged by the way he handled the Bonus Army incident.
    D) Roosevelt's confidence and charisma provided hope for many American voters.

16. During the 1920s, Franklin Roosevelt
    A) married Eleanor.
    B) served as assistant secretary of the navy.
    C) bravely fought back against the ravages of polio.
    D) switched from the Republican to the Democratic Party.

17. In the election of 1932,
    A) third-party candidates played a major role.
    B) Roosevelt won by less than 5% of the vote.
    C) Hoover's active campaigning was a major factor.
    D) Roosevelt won every state south and west of Pennsylvania.

18. Which of the following acts was part of FDR's Hundred Days campaign?
    A) Glass-Steagall Act
    B) Emergency Banking Act
    C) Farm Credit Act
    D) All of the above

19. "The 100 Days" refers to
    A) the active first three months of FDR's first term of office.
    B) the "lame duck" final few months of Hoover's presidency.
    C) the immediate after-effects of the Stock Market crash.
    D) the length of the sitdown strike at Fisher body plant.

20. Franklin Roosevelt's first goal as president was to
    A) strengthen the faltering bank industry.
    B) provide pensions for the elderly.
    C) balance the national government's budget.
    D) cut income taxes for the wealthy.

21. The Federal Emergency Relief Administration
    A) combined work relief work with conservation.
    B) furnished funds to local and state governments.
    C) created a regulatory board for settling labor disputes.
    D) was one of FDR's ideas that was rejected by Congress.

22. Which agency was created personally by FDR and was very popular with the public?
    A) The Wagner-Peyser Act
    D) The Social Security Act
    C) The Farm Credit Administration
    D) The Civilian Conservation Corps

23. The Agricultural Adjustment Administration attempted to
    A) nationalize rail lines that carried farm products.
    B) raise farm incomes by attacking overproduction.
    C) decrease the emphasis on scientific agriculture.
    D) acknowledge farmers' calls for collective bargaining rights.

24. The plight of American farmers during the depression was magnified by
    A) FDR's refusal to develop a comprehensive farm policy.
    B) the Socialist Party's active role in rural politics of the 1930s.
    C) devastating droughts and dust storms throughout the 1930s.
    D) the refusal of large producers to participate in the AAA.

25. The Securities Act
    A) stabilized the private banking system.
    B) established a national system of relief.
    C) required full disclosure from stock exchanges.
    D) guaranteed bank deposits.

When?

Directions- Fill in the letter 'A' if the event took place during FDR's first term or 'B' if the event took place during FDR's second term.

1. _____ AAA created to regulate farm production

2. _____ The Civilian Conservation Corps establishes many jobs in the area of conservation and reforestation projects.

3. _____ The Emergency Banking Act is passed in the effort to stabilize the banking system.

4. _____ The Social Security Act provides old-age pensions for the first time in U.S. history.

5. _____ Congress, with the active support of labor, passes the Wagner Act.

6. _____ AAA ruled unconstitutional

7. _____ The Congress of Industrial Organizations is founded.

8. _____ The Tennessee Valley Authority is created to coordinate regional development.

9. _____ The Supreme Court rules the NRA unconstitutional.

Where?

Matching

Match the following people with their home states.

William Lemke	North Dakota
Francis Townsend	California
Charles Coughlin	Michigan
Huey P. Long	Louisiana
Robert Wagner	New York

How and Why?

1. How did Herbert Hoover's voluntarism fail to solve the problems of the Great Depression?

2. Describe the conflict that led to FDR's proposal that the president be given more power in the organization of the Supreme Court. What were the specifics of FDR's "court packing" proposals?

3. Discuss the ways in which the Depression affected the following groups: African Americans, Hispanics, and Mexicans.

4. Describe the important role that Eleanor Roosevelt played in the American political scene of the 1930s.

5. What factors led to a rift in the American Federation of Labor? How was the Congress of Industrial Organizations different from the A.F.L.?

6. In what ways were Herbert Hoover's economic ideas more progressive than his Republican predecessors in office? Despite these ideas, what political failings caused his demise as president?

7. Discuss and analyze the elements that produced Franklin Roosevelt's landslide victory over Herbert Hoover in the election of 1932.

8. Choose three New Deal relief programs and describe them. What were they designed to accomplish? What were the achievements and/or failings of these programs?

9. Many historians have stated that Franklin Roosevelt was "the right man at the right time." Evaluate the thematic evidence that produces this thesis.

10. Arthur Schlesinger has written that FDR's strengths included his ability to unite the nation against a common foe, and his instinct for finding the "vital center" of American thinking. What historical evidence caused Schlesinger to express this thesis?

11. Do you support those members of the black press who said that the National Recovery Administration (NRA) actually stood for "Negro Run Around" or "Negroes Ruined Again?" Why or why not? Cite specific examples of FDR's reforms for African Americans that either support or refute these slogans.

Chapter 26
World War II, 1939-1945

Practice Test

1. Many scientists who helped develop the atomic bomb for the United States
    A) were hired by the joint authority of the U.S., England, and the Soviet Union.
    B) made it known that they felt the project should not be kept secret.
    C) had escaped from Fascist and Nazi aggression in Europe.
    D) insisted that no one but they be given access to the research building.

2. Which is the correct trio of Axis powers in World War II?
    A) Germany, Japan, Italy
    B) Soviet Union, Germany, Italy
    C) Germany, Italy, France
    D) Soviet Union, Japan, Germany

3. The conquest of which country was termed a 'blitzkrieg'.
    A) Austria
    B) Netherlands
    C) Poland
    D) Balkans

4. The earliest fascist aggression took place when
    A) Hitler created death camps in Eastern Europe.
    B) Japan launched a brutal invasion of China.
    C) Italy attacked and conquered Ethiopia.
    D) the German air force launched raids on Great Britain.

5. Eighty-five percent of Americans
    A) supported continued restrictions on immigration.
    B) believed the nation should fight only if directly attacked.
    C) did not care if either the Allies or Axis powers
       prevailed.
    D) believed that the nation had been wrong to enter World War I.

6. Congress ordered the expansion of the military and an increase in defense production when
    A) England surrendered after the Battle of Dunkirk.
    B) Japan invaded China.
    C) France easily collapsed under Nazi aggression.
    D) the U.S. signed a friendship pact with the Soviet Union in 1936.

7. FDR's "lend-lease" program allowed
   A) states to earn block grants from the federal government.
   B) Britain to borrow military equipment from the U.S.
   C) the U.S. to sell military supplies to the Axis Powers.
   D) minorities to receive equal treatment in New Deal programs.

8. America First was known for its
   A) support of FDR's lend-lease program.
   B) fundraising on behalf of Democratic candidates.
   C) belief that the U.S. should defend its own borders and not its European allies.
   D) contention that the U.S. was letting down democracy by not fighting fascism.

9. What was the name of the US destroyer that clashed with a German submarine and prompted Roosevelt to institute a 'shoot on sight' policy?
   A) Ruben James
   B) Greer
   C) Kearny
   D) Arizona

10. The Atlantic Charter of 1941
    A) created further distance between the U.S. and European involvement.
    B) provided a political framework for the possibility of American involvement.
    C) did not express American opposition to territorial change by conquest.
    D) emphasized the defeat of imperial Japan as the first priority.

11. In the months leading up to Pearl Harbor,
    A) relations between the U.S. and Japan appeared to be getting better.
    B) Germany withdrew its troops from the Soviet Union.
    C) FDR froze Japanese assets and increased U.S. naval presence in the Pacific.
    D) Japan signed a non-aggression pact with China.

12. All of the following statements about Pearl Harbor are true EXCEPT
    A) the American decision to build a "two-ocean navy" made confrontation seem imminent.
    B) FDR had already assumed a firm but defensive policy in the Pacific.
    C) the U.S. had begun to crack Japanese codes, but anticipated an attack in Asia.
    D) Hitler and Mussolini didn't declare war against the U.S. until a year after Pearl Harbor.

13. Which statement about Pearl Harbor is true?
    A) Over 2,000 Americans were killed in the surprise Japanese attack.
    B) Japan destroyed all of the oil storage tanks at Pearl Harbor.
    C) The attack left the U.S. with no naval carriers in the Pacific.
    D) Even after the attack, many Congressmen voted against a declaration of war.

14. A turning point on the Eastern Front came when
    A) the Americans defeated the Japanese navy at the Battle of Midway.
    B) Allied forces defeated the Germans at El Almein.
    C) the Soviet Union forced a German surrender after the Battle of Stalingrad.
    D) FDR sent two million troops to the aid of the battered Soviet Union.

15. A turning point in the Battle of the Atlantic came when
    A) German manufacturers surprisingly stopped producing U-boats.
    B) the Soviet Union sent naval reinforcements.
    C) Admiral Yamomoto realized his forces were outnumbered.
    D) new sonar systems improved tracking of German U-boats.

16. The Allies stopped the German and Italian advance toward the Suez Canal
    A) with a decisive victory at the Battle of El Almein.
    B) despite the fact that the Allies were outnumbered two to one.
    C) when Field Marshal Erwin Rommel surrendered after very little fighting.
    D) as a result of the Germans' defeat at the Battle of Stalingrad.

17. Which of the following occurred last?
    A) The Japanese strike the Philippines, destroying most American air power and isolating U.S. forces.
    B) Japan defeats the combined American, Dutch, British, and Australian fleet.
    C) Japan pushes the British out of Burma.
    D) Corregidor is surrendered to the Japanese.

18. The Allies consisted of:
    A) Germany, Japan, Italy.
    B) U.S., China, Germany.
    C) Germany, Italy, China.
    D) U.S., Britain, the Soviet Union.

19. The first check to Japanese expansion came at the Battle of the Coral Sea when
    A) U.S. aircraft carriers halted a Japanese advance toward Australia.
    B) British reinforcements relieved a battered U.S. navy.
    C) the Japanese were forced to surrender the island fortress of Corregidor.
    D) the alliance of the Axis Powers dissolved.

20. Which statement about American support for World War II is true?
    A) Officials were surprised that not many men enlisted after Pearl Harbor.
    B) For the first time in U.S. military history, racial equality existed in the army.
    C) The support for war unified Americans across regional, national, and class divisions.
    D) Women played no significant role in the Allies' victory.

21. What battle put an end to Japanese efforts to expand in the Pacific?
    A) The Battle of the Coral Sea
    B) The Battle of Midway
    C) The Battle of Aleutian Islands
    D) None of the above

22. The Manhattan Project
    A) was only a theoretical project.
    B) was completed by Enrico Fermi.
    C) ushered in the atomic age.
    D) was applauded and embraced by all the scientists involved in it.

23. The Women's Air Force Service Pilots did all the following EXCEPT
    A) ferried military aircraft across the US.
    B) towed targets for antiaircraft practices.
    C) carried male passengers.
    D) tested new planes.

24. All of the following statements about war production are true EXCEPT
    A) U.S. workers produced a staggering 40% of all war materials in the world.
    B) the great Depression was ended due to the upturn in the wartime economy.
    C) the poorest quarter of Americans were excluded from wartime industries.
    D) existing factories were very effective at retooling for producing war materials.

25. Which Native American tribe was considered "code talkers" in World War II?
    A) Pueblos
    B) Cherokees
    C) Navajos
    D) Sioux

When?

1. Which event happened last?
    A) The Japanese attack Pearl Harbor.
    B) Mussolini overthrown and killed in Italy.
    C) The Germans invade Poland.
    D) Franklin Roosevelt is elected to a third term.

2. What is the correct order of events?
    A) Japan attacks China, America enters the war, D-Day invasion.
    B) D-Day invasion, Japan attacks China, America enters the war.
    C) America enters the war, D-Day invasion, Japan attacks China.
    D) D-Day invasion, America enters the war, Japan attacks China.

3. Which headline would have appeared in 1945?
   A) "Axis Powers Sign Tripartite Pact of Aggression"
   B) "Americans Stop Japanese Advance at Midway"
   C) "Race Riot Plagues Detroit"
   D) "Nation Stunned as it Mourns Loss of FDR"

4. The last military action of World War II was
   A) the Battle of Iwo Jima.
   B) the Allied capture of Berlin.
   C) the atomic bombing of Nagasaki.
   D) the Battle of the Bulge.

5. Which event happened in the 1930s?
   A) Germany invaded the Soviet Union.
   B) The number of women workers in America increased dramatically.
   C) Germany and Italy formed the Rome-Berlin Axis.
   D) Allied forces invaded Normandy.

Where?

Matching

Match the following figures of World War II with the appropriate country.

Adolf Hitler	France
Benito Mussolini	Germany
Francisco Franco	Italy
Neville Chamberlain	Spain
England	

Map Skills

Use Map 26-4 to answer and label the following questions.

1. Name two of the major battles.

2. What two Japanese cites were hit by US airstrikes?

3. Name neutral nations.

4. The battle of Kwajalein took place in which months?

5. The US began its air assault on Japan in what year?

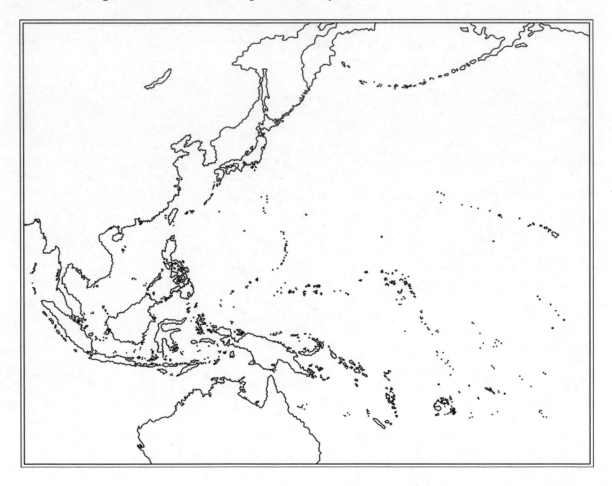

How and Why?

1. What actions illustrate Japanese, German, and Italian aggression in the 1930s?

2. In what ways was FDR preparing for war before the invasion of Pearl Harbor?

3. What evidence reveals the vital role that American manufacturing played in the victory of the Allies?

4. Describe American policy regarding the war in the period 1935 to December 7-8, 1941.

5. How did American unity provide a foundation for success in World War II? Describe examples of Americans on the homefront which illustrate the importance of that unity.

6. What factors combined to produce the defeat of Germany? Be sure to explain the roles of the Soviet Union, the bombing campaigns, and the D-Day invasion in the victory of the Allies.

7. Respond to the following statement: "American entry into World War II emerged as a vital factor in the defeat of the Axis Powers."

8. What evidence reveals the brutal nature of the war in the Pacific? What factors contributed to President Truman's decision to drop the atomic bomb? Of those factors, which one do you think was most influential in his mind?

9. Analyze the wartime experiences of three of the following groups: women, African-Americans, Mexican-Americans and Japanese-Americans, and Native Americans. Did these experiences help or hinder progress toward equality in America?

10. Based on your reading of this chapter, do you believe that FDR wanted an excuse for war or not? Cite specific examples in your response.

Chapter 27
The Cold War at Home and Abroad, 1946-1952

Practice Test

1. The economic expansion that happened in the years of 1947-1948 helped to finance
    A) out of work laborers.
    B) the welfare system.
    C) military buildup and foreign policy.
    D) the Taft-Hartley act.

2. The Employment Act of 1946 did NOT
    A) help define post-war economic growth.
    B) establish a council of economic advisers to assist the president.
    C) attempt to ward off a possible economic crisis.
    D) guarantee full employment for all American workers.

3. The Taft-Hartley Act
    A) represented the most progressive labor reforms since the Wilson
       administration.
    B) was an attempt by big business to reverse gains made by organized labor.
    C) limited immigration of Asians and eastern Europeans.
    D) was successful because it was supported by John L. Lewis.

4. The G.I. Bill was geared at helping veterans in the areas of
    A) housing and education.
    B) mental health and self esteem.
    C) welfare payments and job counseling.
    D) medical care and cash bonuses.

5. One immediate problem in the first few years after the war was
    A) large-scale unemployment.
    B) the national feeling that not much was gained by victory in the war.
    C) a housing shortage.
    D) a marked decrease in the standard of living for the middle class.

6. The FHA
    A) financed nearly 40 percent of all home mortgage debt between 1946-1950.
    B) required that labor leaders take oaths that they were not communists.
    C) began a trend that resulted in rampant inflation during the early 1950s.
    D) supported the third-party candidacy of Henry Wallace in 1948.

7. Levittown represented a change toward
    A) an increase in Americans who owned small farms.
    B) a belief in labor-management equity.
    C) affordable homes in American suburbs.
    D) the development of suburbs based in ethnic identity.

8. Civil rights reforms enacted by the Truman administration included
    A) passage of the Voting Rights Act.
    D) a constitutional amendment to ensure citizenship.
    C) desegregation of all public facilities.
    D) desegregation of the armed forces.

9. The courageous athlete who broke the "color line" in major-league baseball was
    A) Jesse Owens.
    B) Hank Aaron.
    C) Jackie Robinson.
    D) Willie Mays.

10. One trend of the period 1946-1950 was
    A) further segregation in professional sports.
    B) a significant increase in the number of babies being born.
    C) a declining fear in the threat of communism.
    D) a growth of power for organized labor.

11. After the war, middle-class Americans overwhelmingly expressed the desire to
    A) assure peace by developing close relations with the Soviet Union.
    B) have small families and live in remote, rural areas.
    C) establish prosperity after 15 years of depression and war.
    D) include socialist policies in the national political agenda.

12. The vital center
    A) reflected the political reality of the Cold War.
    B) was a book by Harry Truman.
    C) was the platform that secured Truman the presidency.
    D) was the platform the Dixiecrats ran on.

13. Which Progressive candidate cast himself as the prophet for "the century of the common man?"
    A) Strom Thurmond
    B) Henry Wallace
    C) Harry Truman
    D) Thomas Dewey

14. The International Monetary Fund was established
    A) by Great Britain.
    B) to assist nations in maintenance of stable currency.
    C) to include all allies except the USSR.
    D) to halt postwar international trade.

15. The U.S. and U.S.S.R. disputed the Yalta Conference's decrees regarding
    A) free elections in western Europe.
    B) the existence of socialism in the U.S.S.R.
    C) the status of Poland.
    D) the war-guilt clause for World War II.

16. The International Monetary Fund and the World Bank were designed to
    A) ease economic tensions between capitalism and communism.
    B) provide redevelopment loans for the Soviet Union.
    C) allow the United States to be isolationist in its foreign policy.
    D) ensure the U.S.'s central role in the reviving world economy.

17. Who coined the phrase "Iron Curtain"?
    A) Truman
    B) Kennan
    C) Churchill
    D) Jandenberg

18. The content of George Kennan's "long telegram" depicted
    A) a return to the depression if the U.S. did not continue social reforms.
    B) an aggressive U.S.S.R. driven by expansionist communism.
    C) a Republican Party that was not loyal to national goals.
    D) President Truman as ineffective leader in domestic affairs.

19. President Truman and Congress, in 1947, appropriated $400 million to
    A) enact desegregation policies in the South.
    B) rebuild public school systems in poor areas.
    C) fight communism in Greece and Turkey.
    D) support left-wing liberation movements in Africa.

20. Truman brought the 1948 campaign home by all of the following EXCEPT
    A) hammering at the Taft-Hartley Act.
    B) praising the accomplishments of the Democratic administration in the West.
    C) calling the Republican Party the party of small business.
    D) tying Dewey to a number of issues.

21. The main purpose of the Truman Doctrine was to
    A) contain communism by not letting it spread to other nations.
    B) continue support for further labor and social welfare reforms.
    C) regulate the banking industry in hopes of avoiding another depression.
    D) suppress all nationalist movements across the globe.

22. A major effect of the Marshall Plan was
    A) a strengthening of the economic relationship between the U.S. and western Europe.
    B) the political downfall of President Truman.
    C) the communist movement in western Europe gained momentum.
    D) business and labor never supported the political or economic philosophy of the plan.

23. MacArthur tried to change Japan's value system by implementing all the following EXCEPT
    A) social reform.
    B) democratization.
    C) demilitarization.
    D) totalitarianism.

24. The U.S. and other Western nations responded to the Berlin blockade by
    A) ignoring the Soviet Union's awkward attempts at expansionism.
    B) airlifting supplies into the isolated city.
    C) threatening to use nuclear weapons against the Soviet Union.
    D) negotiating with the Soviet Union.

25. The North Atlantic Treaty Organization
    A) solidified ties between the U.S. and its western European allies.
    B) continued the U.S.'s tradition of no entangling alliances.
    C) strengthened political ties, but did not address military matters.
    D) consisted only of the United States, England, and Germany.

When?

1. Which event happened last?
    A) The Rosenberg's were convicted and executed.
    B) Truman established federal employee loyalty program.
    C) Marshall Plan provided economic aid to Europe.
    D) The United States tested the Hydrogen Bomb.

2. HUAC holds Hollywood hearings in what year?
    A) 1944
    B) 1946
    C) 1947
    D) 1950

3. Which headline would have appeared in the 1940s?
    A) "Truman Stuns Pollsters—Rolls to Reelection Over Dewey"
    B) "Truce Talks Begin in Korea"
    C) "McCarthy, Eisenhower Appear Together on Convention Stage"
    D) "Forces of U.S., China Come Face-to-Face in Korea"

4. Which event did NOT occur during the Truman presidency?
    A) the Alger Hiss hearings
    B) the Berlin Airlift overcame Soviet blockade
    C) George Kennan first explains containment policy
    D) McCarthy censured by the Senate

5. Which event happened first?
    A) Truman defeats Dewey
    B) Communist Chinese defeat Nationalists
    C) Alger Hiss convicted of perjury
    D) the United Nations is founded

Where?

Matching

Match the following figures with their home states.

Strom Thurmond	Wisconsin
Hubert Humphrey	Texas
Richard Nixon	Minnesota
Martin Dies	California
Joseph McCarthy	South Carolina

Map Skills

Use Map 27-2 to answer and label the following questions.

1. What was the farthest area the Chinese advanced to?

2. Name the area of farthest advancement of the North Koreans.

3. Which country did the armistice line run through?

4. Name the city farthest northeast that was involved in the conflict.

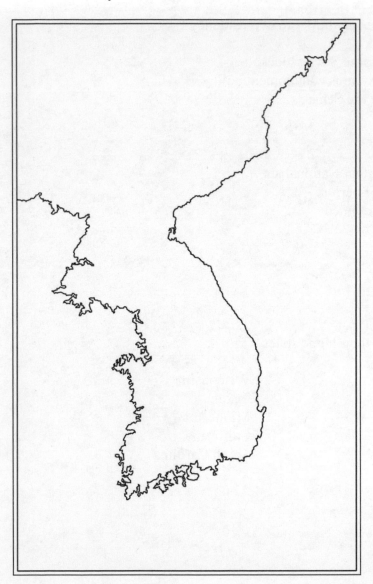

How and Why?

1. Describe the differences between the Democrats and Republicans regarding the legacy of the New Deal in the period 1945-1952.

2. How did the second Red Scare differ from the first? What was the overriding goal of the second Red Scare and was it successful? Why or why not?

3. What were the major objectives expressed in NSC-68?

4. What evidence reveals the existence of consumer and baby booms in the immediate postwar years?

5. How did the Taft-Hartley Act reduce the influence and power of American labor?

6. What combined roles did the Truman administration and the Republican Party play in promoting fear of an internal communist threat?

7. Analyze the causes of Harry Truman's upset victory in the election of 1948. Which factor do you believe was most decisive?

8. Describe the relationship of containment and NSC-68 to the purpose of the American involvement in the Korean War. Do you feel that the U.S. was successful in achieving its goals?

9. What were the causes of the intense fear of communist subversion in the late 1940s and early 1950s? Who were the key figures in the Second Red Scare? What long-term impact did the Red Scare have on American society?

10. Choose three of the following factors that intensified the Cold War and evaluate them:

> NSC-68, Soviet expansionism, American fear of communist infiltration, spy rings, the further development of nuclear weapons, the strategy of containment, the victory of Chinese Communists.

Chapter 28
The Confident Years, 1953-1964

Practice Test

1. The first artificial space satellite was launched by the USSR in
    A) 1952.
    B) 1962.
    C) 1957.
    D) 1950.

2. A key to Dwight Eisenhower's political success was his
    A) close ties with Harry Truman.
    B) promise to undo New Deal reforms.
    C) positive image with both liberals and conservatives.
    D) belief that free trade was harming the economy.

3. Between 1950 and 1964, the American economy
    A) experienced sluggish growth and decline.
    B) grew at a consistent pace.
    C) experienced a depression.
    D) solved the problems of poverty.

4. The Congressional policy of *termination* provided one-time payments, but little else to help
    A) blacks.
    B) women.
    C) Latinos.
    D) Indians.

5. In 1954, Congress focused its housing policy on
    A) family farms.
    B) urban renewal.
    C) better housing for blacks.
    D) building shopping malls.

6. Which statement about urban renewal from 1954-1964 is true?
    A) Rundown housing was often destroyed and replaced with new office buildings, sports arenas, hospitals, and luxury apartments.
    B) Housing problems for the poor were solved in the North.
    C) Small farmers also benefitcd from federal urban renewal funds.
    D) Conservatives used urban renewal to attack the awful level of poverty.

7. The Eisenhower administration used government spending in modernizing
    A) the American medical system.
    B) the national highway system.
    C) the Civilian Conservation Corps.
    D) environmental protection methods.

8. Changes in the domestic economy during the 1950s included
    A) a decrease in the number of franchise businesses.
    B) consumers were more reluctant to buy on credit.
    C) consumers bought more commodities on credit.
    D) a shrinking of the middle class.

9. All of the following were new to consumers in the 1950's EXCEPT
    A) large-scale suburban shopping centers, such as Northgate in Seattle.
    B) franchised hotels and fast-food restaurants, such as Holiday Inn and
       McDonald's.
    C) new environments for high-intensity consumption, such as Disneyland.
    D) mass production of bottled soda pop, such as Coca Cola and 7-Up.

10. Patterns in family living of the 1950s included
    A) children spending more time on the streets than with their families.
    B) pressure on women to pursue husbands rather than professional aspirations.
    C) promotion of the belief that strong families did not defend the U.S. against
       communism.
    D) an increase in the percentage of adults who chose to remain single.

11. Situation-comedy television shows of the 1950s portrayed American families as
    A) unimportant in American culture.
    B) troubled and full of conflict.
    C) including two parents who worked in the professions.
    D) northern European in single-family houses with friendly neighbors.

12. All of the following were part of the basic critique of the ideology of prosperity
EXCEPT
    A) the dissatisfaction of women.
    B) the alienating effects of consumerism.
    C) the conformity of homogenous suburbs
    D) affluence exposed inequality

13. _____ was deemed an antidote to communism in the 1950s.
    A) Film
    B) Religion
    C) A renewed interest in reading
    D) The importance of family

222

14. Who did NOT first rise to great popularity in the 1950s?
    A) The Beatles
    B) Elvis Presley
    C) Richie Valens
    D) Buddy Holly

15. In what year was the phrase "In God we trust" added to US currency?
    A) 1952
    B) 1954
    C) 1955
    D) 1957

16. The phrase "under God" was added to the Pledge of Allegiance in
    A) 1953.
    B) 1954.
    C) 1955.
    D) 1956.

17. The writings of Norman Vincent Peale
    A) criticized the dominance of Protestantism in American culture.
    B) supported passage of further social reform programs.
    C) were judged to be communistic during the McCarthy hearings.
    D) urged positive thinking by combining psychology and religion.

18. All of the following authors wrote books that analyzed America's growing prosperity EXCEPT
    A) John Kenneth Galbraith.
    B) John Foster Dulles.
    C) William H. Whyte Jr.
    D) David Potter.

19. Betty Friedan's famous book was
    A) The Power Elite.
    B) The Other America.
    C) The Feminine Mystique.
    D) The Affluent Society.

20. What country had problems with the United Fruit Company?
    A) Mexico
    B) Guatemala
    C) Honduras
    D) Costa Rica

21. Dwight Eisenhower did all of the following during his two-term presidency EXCEPT
    A) refuse to dismantle successful New Deal programs.
    B) extend American military while avoiding war.
    C) place more emphasis on domestic reforms than foreign affairs.
    D) control information to keep his political opponents guessing.

22. One trend in governmental spending during the 1950s was
    A) a significant increase in defense spending.
    B) cutting all social reform programs.
    C) providing no new educational programs.
    D) a lack of funding for containment efforts.

23. NASA was established to compete with what country's space program?
    A) England
    B) France
    C) Soviet Union
    D) Vietnam

24. The leader of the Vietnamese nationalist movement that toppled French rule was
    A) Ho Chi Minh.
    B) Ngo Dinh Diem.
    C) Syngman Rhee.
    D) Dien Bien Phu.

25. After French rule in Vietnam ended, the U.S.
    A) urged democratic reforms in Vietnam.
    B) signed a non-aggression pact with Vietnamese communists.
    C) backed an authoritarian regime led by pro-western Vietnamese.
    D) attacked communist positions near the Suez Canal.

When?

1. Which event did NOT happen in the 1960s?
    A) the assassination of President Kennedy
    B) Khruschev's US visit
    C) the Gulf of Tonkin Resolution
    D) the Montgomery bus strike

2. Which event happened first?
    A) The Civil Rights Act was passed.
    B) A decision was issued in the *Brown v. Board of Education* case.
    C) A U.S. astronaut orbited the earth for the first time.
    D) Medicare and Medicaid were established.

3. Which headline would have appeared in 1963?
   A) "JFK Edges Nixon in One of Nation's Closest Elections"
   B) "Soviets Successfully Launch Sputnik"
   C) "Quarter-Million Americans Gather to Hear King at Lincoln Memorial"
   D) "Ike Orders Federal Troops to Protect Black Students in Little Rock"

4. Which event happened last?
   A) The Soviets launched Sputnik.
   B) President Johnson signed the Voting Rights Act.
   C) Martin Luther King gave his "I Have a Dream" speech.
   D) Montgomery bus strike.

5. In which election did televised debates play a vital role?
   A) 1948
   B) 1952
   C) 1956
   D) 1960

Where?

Matching

Match the following figures with the appropriate home state.

Adlai Stevenson	Kansas
Lyndon Johnson	Illinois
John Kennedy	Texas
Linda Brown	Massachusetts

Map Skills

Use Map 28-1 to answer and label the following questions.

1. What year was the US Marine landing in the Dominican Republic?

2. What countries are European possessions?

3. When and from what country was Batista overthrown?

4. The US intervened in what country in 1994?

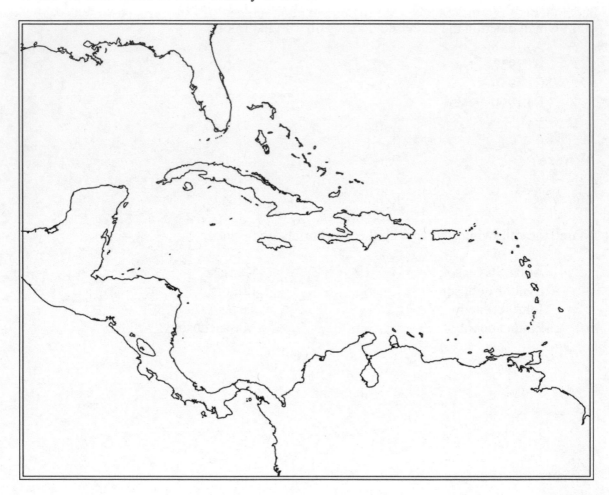

How and Why?

1. How did television portray the American middle-class in the 1950s and early 1960s?

2 What examples reveal that United States foreign policy sometimes involved backing undemocratic regimes in the effort to contain communism?

3. Who was Betty Friedan and why was her book *The Feminine Mystique* viewed as such a ground-breaking piece of writing? What effect did her work have on the art world?

4. What factors contributed to John Kennedy's victory in the election of 1960?

5. What Civil Rights Acts were supported and passed under the leadership of Lyndon Johnson?

6. How did the economic prosperity of the 1950s and early 1960s shape social and political life in the United States?

7. What characteristics and organizations defined the non-violent movement to achieve civil rights in the period 1954-1965? What successes were achieved in this period? Describe who you believe were the most successful leaders of these efforts.

8. In what ways did John Kennedy's mystique shape the national mood of the early 1960s? What successes and failures did JFK experience as president? How did his combination of idealism and shrewdness affect the rest of the 1960s?

9. Describe the ways in which both Dwight Eisenhower and Lyndon Johnson furthered the legacy and reforms of Franklin Roosevelt's New Deal.

10. In 1965, civil-rights leaders consistently expressed that Lyndon Johnson was "the best president that American blacks ever had." What factors caused the leaders to voice this opinion?

Chapter 29
Shaken to the Roots, 1965-1980

Practice Test

1. NOW was founded in
    A) 1962.
    B) 1964.
    C) 1966.
    D) 1967.

2. The *search and destroy* strategy began to fail because
    A) the Chinese sent reinforcements to the aid of North Vietnam.
    B) South Vietnamese guerrillas resembled civilians making it difficult to recognize the enemy.
    C) Congress would not expand use of the military draft.
    D) the U.S. was reluctant to back up infantry detachments with air strikes.

3. The majority of the draftees and enlistees for military service in Vietnam
    A) were college students.
    B) were from working-class families.
    C) averaged about 25 years of age.
    D) came from the Lower South.

4. The Students for a Democratic Society believed all EXCEPT
    A) it was the new left and was free from doctrinal squabbles
    B) called for grassroots action
    C) called for a participatory democracy
    D) war was a result of flaws in American character

5. Mario Savio founded
    A) Students for Democratic Society.
    B) the Free Speech Movement.
    C) the Model Cities Program.
    D) the Selective Service Program.

6. The youth culture was influenced most of all by
    A) films.
    B) philosophy.
    C) poets.
    D) music.

7. Events in the Watts section of Los Angeles in 1965 showed that
    A) racial unrest could result in violent riots.
    B) grass-roots democracy was succeeding by using non-violence.
    C) the power of non-violent civil disobedience was growing.
    D) the Democratic Party was calming the anger of poor Americans.

8. Which statement about riots in urban ghettos in the 1960s is true?
    A) The riots were instigated by outside agitators.
    B) The riots were confined to cities in the South.
    C) Politicians such as Governor Ronald Reagan sympathized with the rioters.
    D) The riots showed the frustrations of residents who had legitimate grievances.

9. The phrase "Black Power" was connected to all of the following EXCEPT
    A) the emphasis of Christian love in civil-rights strategies.
    B) celebrating African-American heritage.
    C) controlling local black communities through political activism.
    D) the messages of speeches given by Stokely Carmichael and Malcolm X.

10. Who coined the phrase 'Black Power'?
    A) Malcolm X
    B) Martin Luther King Jr.
    C) Stokely Carmichael
    D) Huey Newton

11. Where was the Nation of Islam the strongest?
    A) Northern cities
    B) Southwestern cites
    C) Midwest
    D) West Coast

12. Bobby Seale and Huey Newton began the Black Panthers in their home area of
    A) Chicago.
    B) Montgomery, Alabama.
    C) Oakland.
    D) Washington, D.C.

13. All of the following statements about the Black Panthers are true EXCEPT
    A) they focused entirely on national rather than local goals.
    B) they began free breakfast programs in northern ghettos.
    C) stopping police brutality was one of their expressed goals.
    D) their goals were expressed in the creation of a political program.

14. Cesar Chavez led a movement that
     A) condemned anti-union businesses in Texas.
     B) Protected the interests if the agricultural workers of California
     C) rejected local organization and grass-roots democracy.
     D) demanded the return of land to Hispanics in New Mexico.

15. Events of the 1960s revealed that Latino-Americans
     A) rejected assimilation and began to form their own groups.
     B) were not active in the quest for civil rights.
     C) were still members of the lower socio-economic class.
     D) no longer were the victims of discrimination.

16. All of the following statements are true about the American Indian Movement
EXCEPT:
     A) The organization attempted to protect Indians from police brutality.
     B) The organization asserted their distinctiveness amongst American Society
     C) It was part of the group that took over Wounded Knee, South Dakota in 1973.
     D) It aimed to increase economic opportunities for Native Americans.

17. The impact of the Tet Offensive was magnified by all of the following facts EXCEPT
     A) television coverage that appeared to show a Viet Cong victory.
     B) the permanent loss of Saigon due to the Viet Cong's surprise offensive.
     C) U.S. officials had predicted that American armies were near victory.
     D) the U.S. embassy in Saigon was momentarily taken over by guerrillas.

18. President Johnson decided not to run for reelection because
     A) he had become overwhelmed by the war and challenges within his party.
     B) his health made it impossible for him to run.
     C) he had been barely elected in the election of 1964.
     D) he believed that Eugene McCarthy was a better spokesman for domestic
        reform.

19. Which two men were assassinated within months of each other in 1968?
     A) Robert Kennedy and Martin Luther King, Jr.
     B) Martin Luther King, Jr. and John Kennedy
     C) John Kennedy and Malcolm X
     D) Malcolm X and Robert Kennedy

20. Which candidate earned 301 electoral votes in the election of 1968?
     A) Eugene McCarthy
     B) Dick Gregory
     C) Eldridge Cleaver
     D) Richard Nixon

21. The Weather Underground group was named after
    A) A painting by Andy Warhol.
    B) Lyrics from a Bob Dylan song.
    C) a meteorological term.
    D) none of the above.

22. After Richard Nixon's election, it became apparent that
    A) relations with the Soviet Union would worsen.
    B) he did not have a secret plan to end the war.
    C) antiwar protests would immediately decline.
    D) Vice President Agnew would not support Nixon's war policies.

23. Four students were killed by the National Guard at Kent State University during a protest of
    A) Richard Nixon's reelection.
    B) Lyndon Johnson's decision to bomb North Vietnam.
    C) the Gulf of Tonkin resolution.
    D) American bombing of Cambodia.

24. Security adviser Henry Kissinger arranged Richard Nixon's surprising diplomatic trip to
    A) North Vietnam.
    B) China.
    C) England.
    D) North Korea.

25. *Détente* means
    A) friendship.
    B) alliance.
    C) easing of tensions.
    D) safety.

When?

1. All of the following happened in 1968 EXCEPT
    A) the release of the Pentagon Papers.
    B) the assassination of Martin Luther King, Jr.
    C) violence in Chicago at the Democratic Convention.
    D) the assassination of Robert Kennedy.

2. Which event happened last?
    A) the Tet Offensive
    B) four students killed at Kent State
    C) Richard Nixon resigns
    D) American hostages taken in Iran

3. What is the correct order of events?
   A) Tet Offensive, Gulf of Tonkin Resolution, LBJ drops out of presidential race
   B) LBJ drops out of presidential race, Gulf of Tonkin Resolution, Tet Offensive
   C) Gulf of Tonkin resolution, Tet Offensive, LBJ drops out of presidential race
   D) Gulf of Tonkin Resolution, LBJ drops out of presidential race, Tet offensive

4. What headline would have appeared in 1975?
   A) "South Vietnamese Government in Saigon Surrenders"
   B) "Nixon to Announce Resignation Tonight"
   C) "Tet Offensive Stuns Army, American Public"
   D) "Hussein, Begin Sign Historic Accord at Camp David"

5. Which event happened in the 1960s?
   A) Neil Armstrong walked on the Moon.
   B) Richard Nixon resigned.
   C) Jimmy Carter defeated Gerald Ford.
   D) Three Mile Island nuclear leak occurred.

Where?

Matching

Match the following figures with their home states.

Gaylord Nelson	Georgia
Richard Nixon	Massachusetts
Clement Haynsworth	California
Jimmy Carter	Florida
Robert Kennedy	Wisconsin

Map Skills

Use Map 29-1 from your text to answer and label the following questions.

1. Name three major battles of the Tet offensive.

2. Name the capitol of Cambodia.

3. Name three cities along the Ho Chi Minh trail

4. In what body of water did the Maddox incident happen?

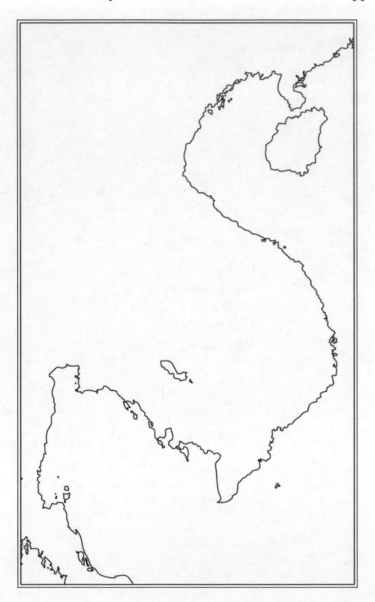

How and Why?

1. Explain the reasons why the *search and destroy* strategy failed in the Vietnam War.

2. What aspects of the military draft fragmented the American public along class lines?

3. What changes did mainstream feminism hope to make in the 1960s? Was this movement successful? Why or why not?

4. What aspects of the 1960s and 1970s revealed the existence of a "generation gap"?

5. What environmental reforms were passed during the Nixon presidency?

6. What causes and events illustrate that 1968 was the most violent year, on the domestic political front, in American history?

7. Discuss the roots and development of "participatory democracy" in the 1960s. What influence would grass-roots democracy have on later American history?

8. What political errors were made regarding American involvement in the Vietnam War? What circumstances led policy-makers to eventually believe that the war could not be won?

9. Analyze the dynamics of the election of 1968. What events, strategies, and factors resulted in Richard Nixon's narrow triumph over Hubert Humphrey?

10. Discuss the connections between the antiwar movement, hippies, the counterculture, and the Black Power movement. What were the successes and failures of the New Left?

Chapter 30
The Reagan Revolution and a Changing World, 1981-1992

Practice Test

1. In the 1980s, immigrants fueled economic growth in all of the following ways EXCEPT
    A) adding a new pool of talent and ambition in the work force.
    B) by revitalizing older neighborhoods.
    C) by changing the ethnic mix of major cities.
    D) by accepting all new immigration laws to avoid rioting.

2. Who was coined the "teflon president"?
    A) Carter
    B) Bush
    C) Reagan
    D) Clinton

3. Neoconservatives such as Edward Banfield believed that
    A) the federal government was spending too much money on defense.
    B) liberal policies failed only because conservatives failed to provide support.
    C) government regulation was more economically effective than promoting free markets.
    D) social problems could not be solved through government policies.

4. The Economic Recovery and Tax Act of 1981 did all of the following things EXCEPT
    A) provide more funds for social welfare programs.
    B) reduce the amount money taken in by the federal government.
    C) attempt to stimulate business activity.
    D) put more money in the hands of consumers.

5. Ronald Reagan's economic plan included all of the following facets EXCEPT
    A) providing less government regulation in big businesses.
    B) enforcing strict protection of natural environments.
    C) reducing taxes on the wealthiest Americans.
    D) encouraging wider participation in the stock market.

6. One effect of deregulation was
    A) the strengthening of organized labor unions.
    B) more economic power for the poor.
    C) the destruction and bail-out of the savings and loan industry.
    D) big business withdrawing its support for President Reagan.

7. *The Bonfire of the Vanities* depicted the socio economic divide between rich and poor America was written by
    A) Bret Easton Ellis
    B) Jay McInerny
    C) Tom Wolfe
    D) Tobias Wolfe

8. The corporate merger mania of the 1980s
    A) helped unions.
    B) hurt unions.
    C) eliminated debt.
    D) helped to stabilize pension funds.

9. "Yuppies" tended
    A) not to reap the economic benefits of the 1980s.
    B) to come from the lowest economic sectors.
    C) not to emulate the upper class in their lifestyles.
    D) to purchase items from upscale retailers.

10. Federal tax and spending policies of the 1980s made life more difficult for
    A) wealthy corporations.
    B) middle-class workers caught in industrial restructuring.
    C) people seeking employment in Sunbelt cities.
    D) the wealthiest members of American society.

11. Which statement about the American poor is NOT true?
    A) The percentage of poor people had decreased in the period 1960-1973.
    B) In the 1980s, there was an increase in the number of Americans living in poverty.
    C) Homelessness was less visible in the 1980s and affected only a handful of Americans.
    D) Analysts referred to an *underclass* who were left out of the economic mainstream.

12. Whose watchword was *prudence*?
    A) Dukakis
    B) Bush
    C) Reagan
    D) Clinton

13. Evidence of a renewed Cold War in the 1980s included all of the following EXCEPT
    A) the American public's belief that the government had been infiltrated by communists.
    B) the U.S.'s placement of of new cruise missiles in Europe.
    C) the belief, expressed in NSD D-13, that a nuclear war was winnable.
    D) a significant increase in the nuclear arms race.

14. In 1982, nearly a million people turned out in New York for a rally
    A) against the Vietnam War.
    B) in support of American offensives in the Persian Gulf War.
    C) in support of a freeze on the development of nuclear weapons.
    D) against Richard Nixon's policies of detente.

15. President Reagan's Strategic Defense Initiative
    A) was defeated in the House of Representatives.
    B) was opposed by heads of the defense industry.
    C) emphasized the use of traditional weapons rather nuclear arsenals.
    D) created an expensive defense plan based on superlasers and satellites.

16. Small-scale American intervention in Lebanon resulted in
    A) a surrender by PLO forces in that region.
    B) the death of over 200 Marines in one bombing incident.
    C) a peace treaty signed by Israel and the PLO.
    D) building trust between the U.S. and the U.S.S.R.

17. The United States invaded Nicaragua to overthrow what group of rebels?
    A) the Contras
    B) the "freedom fighters"
    C) the Sandinistas
    D) none of the above

18. In the Iran-Contra affair, Oliver North
    A) testified that President Reagan was solely to blame.
    B) was innocent of any unconstitutional actions.
    C) funneled illegal arms sales funds to Nicaraguan rebels.
    D) was completely honest in his testimony.

19. Which statement about the Iran-Contra affair is NOT true?
    A) President Reagan and Vice President were unaware of any wrongdoings.
    B) The Reagan administration defied its trade embargo with Iran.
    C) The arms deal contradicted the U.S.'s claim that it wouldn't negotiate with
       terrorists.
    D) Many illegal activities were involved in the arms-for-hostages dealings.

20. Which Soviet leader instituted the political openness of *glasnost*?
    A) Yuri Andropov
    B) Leonid Brezhnev
    C) Constantin Chernenko
    D) Mikhail Gorbachev

21. President Reagan reacted to Mikhail Gorbachev's offers of Soviet military cutbacks
    A) with great suspicion.
    B) by refusing to meet with the Soviet leader.
    C) by embracing the Soviet Union's new positions.
    D) after Gorbachev was removed from office.

22. Supporters of the International Nuclear Force agreement did NOT include
    A) Secretary of State George Schultz.
    B) American peace activists.
    C) President Reagan.
    D) chief advisers of the CIA.

23. George H.W. Bush viewed diplomacy
    A) in personal terms, influencing relations with the Soviets under Gorbachev.
    B) in terms of the traditional view of reconciling national interests.
    C) as unimportant in the modern world of foreign policy.
    D) as not being part of the president's responsibilities.

24. Who founded the Rainbow Coalition?
    A) Pat Buchanan
    B) Pat Robertson
    C) Jesse Jackson
    D) Dan Quayle

25. By the end of 1989, there were new non-communistic governments in all of the following countries EXCEPT
    A) Romania.
    B) Bulgaria.
    C) East Germany.
    D) Yugoslavia.

When?

1. Which event happened last?
    A) President Reagan was reelected.
    B) Germans tore down the Berlin wall.
    C) America and its allies won the Persian Gulf War.
    D) 241 Marines were killed by a terrorist bomb in Lebanon.

2. Which headline would have appeared in 1992?
    A) "U.S. Invades Granada"
    B) "Regan Wins a Second Term"
    C) "Officers Acquitted in the Beating of Rodney King"
    D) "Iraq Invades Kuwait"

3. Which event did NOT happen in the 1990s?
   A) Riots flared after the police were acquitted in Rodney King beating.
   B) President Clinton was elected to a first term.
   C) Corruption was revealed in Iran-Contra affair.
   D) Republicans announced "Contract with America."

4. In what year did the Soviet Union dissolve into independent nations?
   A) 1980
   B) 1988
   C) 1991
   D) 1996

5. Which event happened first?
   A) George Bush elected president.
   B) Oliver North testified before Senate committee.
   C) U.S. allies defeated Iraq in the Persian Gulf War.
   D) The Senate approved the nomination of Clarence Thomas to the Supreme Court.

Where?

Matching

Match the following figures with the country with which they are associated.

Ayatollah Khomeini	United States
Boris Yeltsin	Iran
Saddam Hussein	Germany
Helmut Kohl	Iraq
Rodney King	Russia

Map Skills

Use Map 30-2 to answer and label the following questions.

1. In what areas were boom cities most common?

2. Name the three states containing metropolitan areas that lost population in the 1990s.

3. Which city in Colorado showed more growth- Denver or Colorado Springs?

4. Name three states where areas of growth were between 20-29 percent.

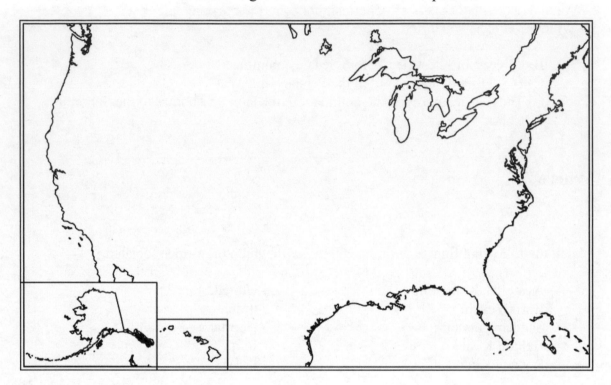

How and Why?

1. Describe the differences of opinion that existed between supporters of a nuclear freeze and advocates of the Strategic Defense Initiative.

2. What were the major goals of American policy in the Persian Gulf War?

3. Define the terms *perestroika* and *glasnost* and describe their impact on relations between the U.S. and the U.S.S.R.

4. How did voters differ in their approach to the issues in the elections of 1980 and 1992?

5. Trace the precedents and explain the foundation of the Supreme Court's decision in *Roe v. Wade.*

6. In what ways did Ronald Reagan's presidency change the economic realities for workers and business corporations? How did federal economic policies of the 1980s affect the lives of the poorest and richest Americans?

7. In what ways did gender become a more powerful political factor in the 1980s and 1990s? Why did minority voters strongly support the Democrats in the elections of 1992 and 1996?

8. What examples reveal conservative political trends in the 1990s? Describe the differences between centrist, neoliberal, and neoconservative visions of America.

9. How did lifting quotas affect immigration reform? What other factors contributed to the large influx of immigrants in the 1970s-1990s?

10. Critics have questioned whether Regan planned an economic revolution or simply presided over changes initiated by others. Based on your reading of the chapter, what do you think? Cite three specific examples to support your reasons.

Chapter 31
Complacency and Crisis, 1993-2003

Practice Test

1. The Clinton/Gore ticket in 1992 won with what percent of the popular vote?
    A) 52
    B) 48
    C) 43
    D) 72

2. The character of the United States in the 1990s embodied
    A) a commitment to ending the Cold War.
    B) foreign policy concerns.
    C) a focus on down-to-earth issues.
    D) a lean to the Left.

3. In the November 1992 election, which of the following did voters rank as the number one issue of concern?
    A) the federal budget deficit
    B) foreign policy
    C) health care
    D) the economy

4. The Contract with America was proposed by
    A) George W. Bush.
    B) Bill Clinton.
    C) Robert Dole.
    D) Newt Gingrich.

5. To curtail the use of firearms, Democrats advocated
    A) stricter mandatory prison terms for those who owned guns.
    B) tighter gun control laws.
    C) the ban of assault weapons.
    D) only government organized militia could purchase guns.

6. The _____ was the biggest contributing factor for the increase in prison population in the 1990s.
    A) lax gun control laws
    B) war on drugs
    C) lack of government interest in crime measures
    D) none of the above

7. What final incident caused the Republican majority in the House Judiciary Committee to recommend the impeachment of Bill Clinton?
    A) Whitewater
    B) appointing Hillary as head of the health-care task force
    C) his inability to make a decision
    D) lying about his affair with Monica Lewinsky

8. From the early 1990s 2000, Americans experienced prosperity because of all of the following EXCEPT
    A) the soaring stock market.
    B) the start of Internet firms.
    C) new growth in the high-tech market.
    D) massive business expansion in the West.

9. Which worker is NOT considered a service worker?
    A) waitress
    B) child-care worker
    C) teacher
    D) go-go dancer

10. How did CNN change the way Americans watched TV?
    A) they broadcasted worldwide
    B) they broadcasted 24-hours a day
    C) the brought instant information to viewers
    D) all of the above

11. The Internet was originally intended to
    A) allow navigation of the World Wide Web.
    B) connect universities with national weapons laboratories.
    C) make communication easier and quicker.
    D) be a communication system to survive a nuclear attack.

12. NAFTA created a "common market" among all of the following EXCEPT
    A) Canadians.
    B) Europeans.
    C) Mexicans.
    D) U.S. Consumers.

13. Which group did NOT oppose NAFTA?
    A) organized labor
    B) environmentalists
    C) communities hit by industrial shutdowns
    D) professional businesses

14. Protestors of the WTO were convinced that the organization
   A) raised net production in the world economy.
   B) made more wealth available to developing nations.
   C) benefited only wealthy nations.
   D) would distribute wealth evenly.

15. Which state experienced the largest percentage of population growth according to the 2000 census?
   A) Massachusetts
   B) Florida
   C) Nevada
   D) California

16. Who made up the fastest growing group in American population in 2000?
   A) Asians
   B) Hispanics
   C) American Indian
   D) African Americans

17. Who was Clinton's Secretary of State?
   A) Madeline Albright
   B) Ruth Bader Ginsburg
   C) Janet Reno
   D) Condoleezza Rice

18. Douglas Wilder from _____ was the first African American governor since the Reconstruction.
   A) North Carolina
   B) South Carolina
   C) Virginia
   D) Mississippi

19. Proposition 187 presented in California in 1994
   A) provided access to public education.
   B) gave unlimited access to health care for immigrants.
   C) closed borders to illegal immigrants.
   D) cut off health care and education for undocumented citizens.

20. Which statement about affirmative action is true?
   A) It espoused non-discrimination.
   B) It focused on quotas.
   C) It was an unfair business practice.
   D) It was started by the Clinton administration.

21. In Florida, which group was turned away from voting in the 2000 election in disproportionate numbers?
    A) Hispanics
    B) Asian Americans
    C) Native Americans
    D) African Americans

22. The outcome of the 2000 election show that the nation
    A) favored strong Republican values.
    B) favored strong Democratic values.
    C) was extremely diverse in its opinions.
    D) was moving toward a strong center.

23. The Bush administration declined to sign all of the following treaties/negotiations EXCEPT for
    A) a new International Criminal Court.
    B) the Kyoto Agreement.
    C) the Convention of Biological Warfare.
    D) a revived Strategic Defense Initiative.

24. Which country is NOT part of the "axis of evil"?
    A) Iran
    B) Saudi Arabia
    C) Iraq
    D) North Korea

25. Many Arabs view the United States as
    A) a negotiator in Arab affairs.
    B) a peacekeeper.
    C) an enemy of Arab nations.
    D) an ally of Arab nations.

When?

1. Which event happened last?
    A) Clinton was acquitted of impeachment charges.
    B) The U.S. Patriot Act was passed.
    C) The World Wide Web was launched.
    D) Paula Jones's lawsuit was dismissed.

2. In what year did crime levels reach their peak?
    A) 1990
    B) 1991
    C) 1992
    D) 1993

3. Which cable channel was the first to change the way America listened to music?
    A) VH-1
    B) Nickelodeon
    C) MTV
    D) CNN

4. What headline would have appeared in 2000?
    A) "Clinton to Run Again?"
    B) "The Taliban Has Seen Its Last Days"
    C) "Bush Defeats Gore"
    D) Congress Slashes Taxes for the Next 10 Years"

5. In what year did Generation Xers come into the political arena?
    A) early 1990s
    B) mid 1990s
    C) late 1990s
    D) early 2000

Where?

Matching

Match the following figures with the city they're associated.

Carl Stokes	Los Angeles
Tom Bradley	Denver
Frederico Pena	Cleveland
Henry Cisneros	San Antonio

Map Skills

Use Map 31-2 to answer and label the following questions.

1. Which areas of the country were more welcoming of women owned business?

2. Name three states which had the lowest percentages of women owned business

3. Name three states which had the highest percentages of women owned business

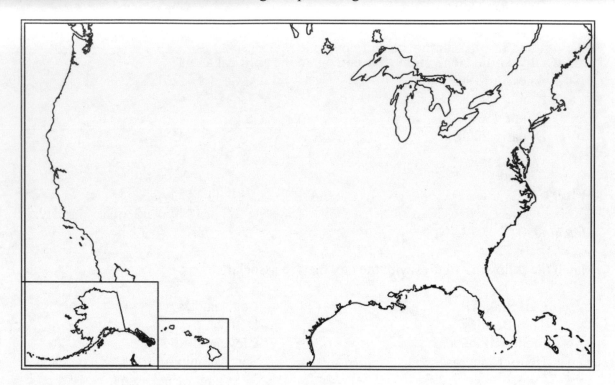

How and Why?

1. In what ways were the views of George Bush and Bill Clinton similar and dissimilar?

2. Analyze the dynamics of the presidential election of 1992. What were the key factors that resulted in Bill Clinton's victory over George Bush?

3. Compare and contrast the visions of America expressed by George Bush, Sr., Bill Clinton, and George W. Bush. Which view is closest to your vision of America? Explain why?

4. The 1990s saw the growth of the Instant Society. What was the instant society? What spurred its growth? Cite 3 specific examples that illustrate how this instant society has changed the way we live our lives.

5. Discuss Clinton's neoliberalism and how it took a two-pronged approach during his first term in office.

6. Do you believe President Clinton should have been removed from office after the Monica Lewinsky incident? Why or why not?

7. Discuss the ways our lives have changed since the attacks on September 11, 2001.

8. Do you support Affirmative Action? Why or why not? In your opinion, does Affirmative Action help or hurt minorities? If possible, use your text to support you opinion.

9. How did the entry of women and minorities into Congress change the face of government?

10. After the events of September 11, 2001, patriotism has come to the forefront of American culture. What is patriotism? How have Americans displayed their new-found patriotism and why do you think it's been embraced to the degree it has been?

LECTURE COMPANION

The following lecture note pages can be used to record your instructor's lectures and assignments for each chapter.

Chapter 16
Reconstruction, 1865-1877

Lecture Notes   **Date:**_____

Chapter 17
A New South, 1877-1900

Lecture Notes Date:_____

Chapter 18
Industry, Immigrants, and Cities, 1870-1900

Lecture Notes   **Date:**_____

Chapter 19
Transforming the West, 1865-1890

Lecture Notes   **Date:**_____

Chapter 20
Politics and Government, 1877-1900

Lecture Notes   Date:_____

Chapter 21
The Progressive Era, 1900-1917

Lecture Notes   **Date:**_____

Chapter 22
Creating an Empire, 1865-1917

Lecture Notes   **Date:**_____

Chapter 23
America and the Great War, 1914-1920

Lecture Notes   **Date:**_____

Chapter 24
Toward a Modern America, The 1920s

Lecture Notes   **Date:**_____

Chapter 25
The Great Depression and the New Deal, 1929-1939

Lecture Notes   **Date:**_____

Chapter 26
World War II, 1939-1945

Lecture Notes   **Date:**_____

Chapter 27
The Cold War at Home and Abroad, 1946-1952

Lecture Notes   **Date:**_____

Chapter 28
The Confident Years, 1953-1964

Lecture Notes   **Date:**_____

Chapter 29
Shaken to the Roots, 1965-1980

Lecture Notes   **Date:**_____

Chapter 30
The Reagan Revolution and a Changing World, 1981-1992

Lecture Notes   **Date:**_____

Chapter 31
Complacency and Crisis, 1993-2003

Lecture Notes

Date:_____

Answer Key (Volume II)

CHAPTER 16: RECONSTRUCTION

Practice Test
1. d
2. c
3. c
4. c
5. a
6. c
7. d
8. b
9. c
10. a
11. a
12. d
13. a
14. c
15. c
16. b
17. b
18. b
19. b
20. d
21. c
22. b
23. d
24. b
25. d

When?
1. d
2. c
3. c
4. c
5. c

Where?
Thaddeus Stevens—Pennsylvania
Charles Sumner—Massachusetts
Martha Schofield—South Carolina
William Tweed—New York

Map Skills
1. Virginia, North Carolina, Mississippi, Georgia, Louisiana
2. 3
3. Tennessee
4. South Carolina, Louisiana, Florida

CHAPTER 17: A NEW SOUTH

Practice Test
1. a
2. c
3. d
4. b
5. c
6. c
7. d
8. b
9. a
10. d
11. b
12. d
13. b
14. c
15. d
16. b
17. c
18. a
19. c
20. b
21. a
22. b
23. b
24. c
25. d

When?
1. d
2. a
3. d
4. c
5. c

Where?
John Pemberton—Georgia
Ida B. Wells—Tennessee
Lily Hammond—Georgia
W.E.B. DuBois—Massachusctts
Charles Macune—Wisconsin

Map Skills
Anwers will vary

CHAPTER 18: INDUSTRY, IMMIGRANTS AND CITIES

Practice Test
1. a
2. c
3. c
4. d
5. d
6. b
7. b
8. d
9. a
10. c
11. b
12. b
13. d
14. a
15. a
16. c
17. d
18. b
19. d
20. b
21. a
22. a
23. a
24. d
25. c

When?
1. c
2. a
3. b
4. d
5. a

Where?
Thomas Edison—New Jersey
Elihu Thompson—Pennsylvania
John D. Rockefeller—New York
Daniel Hale Williams—Illinois
Ella Russell—New Jersey

Map Skills
1. San Francisco
2. New Orleans
3. New York
4. St. Louis
5. San Francisco

CHAPTER 19: TRANSFORMING THE WEST

Practice Test
1. b
2. a
3. b
4. a
5. d
6. c
7. d
8. b
9. b
10. d
11. a
12. c
13. b
14. c
15. b
16. a
17. b
18. d
19. c
20. c
21. a
22. c
23. c
24. b
25. b

When?
1. a

2. b
3. d
4. c
5. b

Where?
Promontory Point—Utah
Wounded Knee—South Dakota
Chisholm Trail—Texas
Bozeman Trail—Montana
Coeur d'Alende—Idaho

Map Skills
1. Southern Pacific
2. Oklahoma
3. Virginia City, Goldhill
4. Montana, North Dakota, Minnesota
5. Black Hills

CHAPTER 20: POLITICS AND GOVERNMENT

Practice Test
1. d
2. d
3. c
4. a
5. a
6. c
7. c
8. a
9. c
10. d
11. b
12. b
13. c
14. a
15. d
16. d
17. c
18. b
19. b
20. b
21. a
22. d
23. d

24. b
25. a

When?
1. c
2. a
3. a
4. b
5. c
6. c
7. c

Matching
James Garfield—Ohio
William McKinley—Ohio
Benjamin Harrison—Indiana
Jacob Coxey—Ohio
Richard Croker—New York

Map Skills
1. South and West
2. Southwest
3. 294,289
4. No

CHAPTER 21: THE PROGRESSIVE ERA

Practice Test
1. b
2. b
3. d
4. c
5. a
6. b
7. b
8. b
9. d
10. b
11. c
12. a
13. c
14. b
15. c
16. b
17. b

18. d
19. c
20. c
21. b
22. d
23. b
24. d
25. d

When?
1. c
2. a
3. b
4. a
5. c
6. a
7. b
8. c
9. c
10. c

Where?
Francis Kellor—New York
Samuel Jones—Ohio
Hoke Smith—Gerogia
Washington Gladden—Ohio
Robert La Follette—Wisconsin

Map Skills
1. 1890s
2. Acadia
3. Denali
4. Arizona-Uteck
5. Yellowstone

CHAPTER 22: CREATING AN EMPIRE

Practice Test
1. a
2. d
3. d
4. d
5. c
6. c
7. d

8. d
9. c
10. c
11. b
12. c
13. c
14. b
15. a
16. a
17. c
18. d
19. d
20. b
21. a
22. b
23. c
24. d
25. d

When?
1. a
2. d
3. d
4. b
5. a
6. b
7. a
8. c

Where?
Henry Cabot Lodge—Massachusetts
Queen Liliuokalani—Hawaii
George Vest—Missouri
John Mitchell—Virginia
Emilio Aguinaldo—Philippines

Map Skills
1. 10
2. 1914
3. France
4. 1903
5. 1898

CHAPTER 23: AMERICA AND THE GREAT WAR

Practice Test
1. a
2. d
3. a
4. a
5. d
6. b
7. c
8. d
9. d
10. c
11. b
12. c
13. d
14. b
15. a
16. a
17. a
18. d
19. c
20. b
21. a
22. c
23. b
24. d
25. d

When?
1. a
2. b
3. a
4. d
5. d

Where?
Kaiser Wilhelm II—Germany
Arthus Zimmerman—Germany
Archduke Franz Ferdinand—Austria
        Hungary
Joseph Joffre—France
V.I. Lenin—Russia

Map Skills
1. Netherlands, Luxemburg, Switzerlans
2. Ypres
3. Cantigny- May 28, 1918
4. Meuse-Argonne

CHAPTER 24: TOWARD A MODERN AMERICA

Practice Test
1. b
2. c
3. d
4. c
5. c
6. a
7. a
8. c
9. a
10. b
11. c
12. b
13. d
14. c
15. b
16. a
17. d
18. d
19. c
20. b
21. b
22. b
23. d
24. a
25. b

When?
1. c
2. a
3. b
4. a
5. c

Where?
Country Club Plaza—Kansas City
Royce Hailey's Pig Stand—Dallas

Yankees—New York
Ford Motor Company—Detroit
Al Capone's Army—Chicago

Map Skills
1. Oklahoma, South Dakota, Kansas and Nebraska
2. Moderate
3. Idaho, Montana, Kentucky, etc.
4. North Carolina, Louisiana, Mississippi, Alabama, Florida
5. New York, Baltimore, Chicago, Detroit, St. Louis

CHAPTER 25: THE GREAT DEPRESSION AND THE NEW DEAL

Practice Test
1. b
2. c
3. b
4. a
5. d
6. c
7. a
8. a
9. b
10. a
11. c
12. d
13. c
14. d
15. b
16. c
17. d
18. d
19. a
20. a
21. b
22. d
23. b
24. c
25. c

When?
1. a

2. a
3. a
4. a
5. a
6. a
7. b
8. a
9. b

Where?
William Lemke—North Dakota
Francis Townsend—California
Charles Coughlin—Michigan
Huey P. Long—Louisiana
Robert Wagner—New York

CHAPTER 26: WORLD WAR II

Practice Test
1. c
2. a
3. c
4. c
5. b
6. c
7. b
8. c
9. b
10. b
11. c
12. d
13. a
14. c
15. d
16. a
17. d
18. d
19. a
20. c
21. b
22. c
23. c
24. c
25. c

When?

1. b
2. a
3. d
4. c
5. c

Where?
Adolf Hitler—Germany
Benito Mussolini—Italy
Francisco Franco—Spain
Neville Chambelain—England

Map Skills
1. Answers may vary- Iwo Jima
Bougainville
2. Osaka, Tokyo
3. Soviet Union; Mongolia
4. January/ February
5. 1944

CHAPTER 27: THE COLD WAR AT HOME AND ABROAD

Practice Test
1. c
2. d
3. b
4. a
5. c
6. a
7. c
8. d
9. c
10. b
11. c
12. a
13. b
14. b
15. c
16. d
17. c
18. b
19. c
20. c
21. a
22. a
23. d
24. b
25. a

When?
1. d
2. c
3. a
4. d
5. d

Where?
Strom Thurmond—South Carolina
Hubert Humphrey—Minnesota
Richard Nixon—California
Martin Dies—Texas
Joseph McCarthy—Wisconsin

Map Skills
1. South of Samchock
2. South of Taegu
3. North Korea
4. Chongjin

CHAPTER 28: THE CONFIDENT YEARS

Practice Test
1. c
2. c
3. b
4. d
5. b
6. a
7. b
8. c
9. d
10. b
11. d
12. d
13. b
14. a
15. c
16. b
17. d
18. b

19. c
20. b
21. c
22. a
23. c
24. a
25. c

When?
1. b
2. b
3. c
4. b
5. d

Where?
Adlai Stevenson—Illinois
Lyndon Johnson—Texas
John Kennedy—Massachusetts
Linda Brown—Kansas

Map Skills
1. 1965
2. Bahamas, Leeward, and Windward Island
3. 1959
4. Haiti

CHAPTER 29: SHAKEN TO THE ROOTS

Practice Test
1. c
2. b
3. b
4. d
5. b
6. d
7. a
8. d
9. a
10. c
11. a
12. c
13. a
14. b

15. a
16. c
17. b
18. a
19. a
20. d
21. b
22. b
23. d
24. b
25. c

When?
1. a
2. d
3. c
4. a
5. a

Where?
Nelson—Wisconsin
Nixon—California
Haynsworth—Florida
Carter—Georgia
Kennedy—Massachusetts

Map Skills
1. answers will vary
2. Phnom Pehn
3. Vihn, Dong Hoi, Khe Sanh
4. Gulf of Tonkin

CHAPTER 30: THE REAGAN REVOLUTION AND A CHANGING WORLD

Practice Test
1. d
2. c
3. d
4. a
5. b
6. c
7. c
8. b
9. d

10. b
11. c
12. b
13. a
14. c
15. d
16. b
17. c
18. c
19. a
20. d
21. c
22. d
23. a
24. c
25. d

When?
1. c
2. c
3. c
4. c
5. c

Where?
Ayatolla Khomeini—Iran
Boris Yeltzin—Russia
Saddam Hussein—Iraq
Helmut Kohl—Germany
Rodney King—United States

Map Skills
1. South east, south west, west coast
2. Ohio, Pennsylvania, New York
3. Same
4. Answers will vary

CHAPTER 31: COMPLACENCY AND
CRISIS

Practice Test
1. c

2. c
3. d
4. d
5. b
6. b
7. d
8. d
9. d
10. b
11. d
12. b
13. d
14. c
15. c
16. b
17. a
18. c
19. d
20. a
21. d
22. c
23. d
24. b
25. c

When?
1. b
2. b
3. c
4. c
5. b

Where?
Carl Stokes—Cleveland
Tom Bradley—Los Angeles
Frederico Pena—Denver
Henry Cisneros—San Antonio

Map Skills
1. West/Great Lakes
2. Answers will vary
3. Answers will vary